THE RAILWAY TOWN OF RAMSBOTTOM

THE RAILWAY TOWN OF RAMSBOTTOM

Past and Present

NIGEL JEPSON

YOUCAXTON
PUBLICATIONS

Copyright © Nigel Jepson 2023

The author asserts the moral right to be identified as the author of this work.
ISBN Number 978-1-915972-26-2

Published by YouCaxton Publications 2023

All rights reserved. No part of this publication may be reproduced, stored in a retrieval system, or transmitted in any form or by any means, electronic, mechanical, photocopying, recording or otherwise, without the prior permission of the author.

This book is sold subject to the condition that it shall not, by way of trade or otherwise, be lent, resold, hired out or otherwise circulated without the author's prior consent in any form of binding or cover other than that in which it is published and without a similar condition including this condition being imposed on the subsequent purchaser.

YouCaxton Publications
www.youcaxton.co.uk

Front cover: top photo shows the last day of the Peel Bridge Tollgate; Friday 26th October 1900 (RHS collection). The bottom photo is Ramsbottom Station today (A.White).

Acknowledgements

Thanks to all the following who have provided invaluable assistance to the project in a variety of ways: Chris Aspin, John Simpson, Philip Dunne, Bob Hargreaves, Mike Kelly, Lee Kenny and Tracey Parkinson, John Brandrick, Jill Clough, James Lawrence, Judith Hilton, Andy Coward, Peter Duncan, David Flood, Alan Garside and John Walker, Wendy Gradwell, Andy Hardman, Linda Henderson, Richard and Chandra Law, Margaret and Dave Wilson, Keith Whitmore, David Wright plus a thank you to members of Ramsbottom Heritage Society: John Leyland, Brenda Richards, Kate Slingsby, Janet Smith, Keith Burroughs. Special gratitude to Andrew Todd, not only on account of tapping into what he has written himself on the topic to date but also for so often being willing to meet up at Rammy café '*Drinc*' to discuss various aspects of local history, including progress of this study.

Useful information regarding the writing of the book was gained courtesy of the *National Railway Museum* in York and the *Science Museum* in London. Acknowledgement and thanks also to Bury, Ramsbottom and Rawtenstall Libraries and Local History resource sections.

In addition, appreciation to Bob Fowke and Ella Knight of 'YouCaxton Press' for their helpful and highly constructive input into the production of this book.

Last but certainly not least, enormous gratitude to my wife Anna for her unstinting assistance and back-up - especially technological.

Photo acknowledgements:

First series: JS Perring – Wikipedia; Tollgate, View from Bridge Street, J&J Whittaker – all Ramsbottom Heritage Society Collection; Station in 1954 – HC Casserly; Cottrill's, photo of original station taken in the 1960s – both RHS Collection; View from level crossing – John Alsop Collection; Beeching – *The Mirror*; Summerseat 1967 – *'Disused Stations'* website; May 1972 – WA Cornwell from Mark Bartlett Collection; Last passenger train 1972 – Chris Totty; State of station in June 1984 – Andrew Todd; Breaking through barrier, Crowds cheering 'return', Station masters meet up, *Gothenburg* and *ELR1* – all Peter Duncan; Grant Clan Pipers – RHS Collection.

Second series: Brooksbottom Viaduct – Peter Duncan; Nuttall Tunnel – Malcolm Orrett, courtesy of Peter Duncan; Newly-reopened signal box – Andy Coward; Peter Duncan and David Steele at work on signalling installations – Andrew Todd; Brian Almond – *The Mirror*; *Leander* 2007 – Paul Anderson; *Tour of Britain* – Pat Kilner; *Thomas the Tank Engine* - ELR; Grants crest – John Leyland; David and Margaret Wilson, Andrew Todd – both photos Anna White; Passing over of 'pouch' – D. Robinson; Ramsbottom station today, the author standing alongside Flying Scotsman – both photos Anna White; Richard Law – *Lancashire Evening Telegraph*; Chandra Law – Richard Law; *Flying Scotswomen* – ELR; The bell from the original station – Jill Clough.

Contents

1. Transport in the area before the advent of railways — 1
2. 'Alarming riot' of rail workers at the *Grant Arms* — 7
3. Ramsbottom becomes Railway Town in 1846 — 17
4. Runaway trains and company rivalry — 28
5. Part of the Lancashire & Yorkshire Railway up to 1923 — 37
6. *Wakes Weeks* excursions and arrival of evacuees at start of World War II — 55
7. Taking a hit from the *'Beeching Cuts'* of the 1960s — 67
8. *'Heaven-sent opportunity'*: opening of the ELR heritage line in 1987 — 77
9. *Teddy Bear Picnics, Thomas the Tank Engine* and *Santa Specials* — 102
10. Pride in maintaining Ramsbottom and Summerseat stations — 115
11. Covid – during and after — 124
12. Postscript — 137
13. Sources — 145
14. Forthcoming Publication — 148

Maps & Diagrams

- At start of Chapter 2: map showing Ramsbottom as part of the mid-19th century rail network from 'Accrington and Bacup to Clifton Junction' – acknowledgements to Andrew Young.
- At start of Chapter 4: East Lancashire Railway - Bury to Rawtenstall - Gradient Profile.
- At start of Chapter 5: map of Ramsbottom Station and its surrounding town area at the beginning of the 20th century.
- At start of Chapter 9: Ramsbottom as part of the modern-day East Lancashire Railway heritage line from Heywood to Rawtenstall.

Introduction

It is now more than thirty-five years ago since the railway line between Bury and Ramsbottom re-opened in 1987. Since that time, Ramsbottom has flourished as a tourist centre on the East Lancashire Railway heritage line, presently operating along a rail track over twelve miles long between Rawtenstall and Heywood.

This book tells the story of how the original East Lancashire Railway first came into being in the 1840s as a result of local Bury and Rossendale businessmen combining to set up a company. Although it took only three years between this first meeting and the opening of a line joining up Bury, Ramsbottom and Rawtenstall, its construction was not without its tensions such as an 'alarming riot' which took place between rival groups of 'navvies' at the *Grant Arms* in Ramsbottom.

The original ELR was destined to have a hectic but relatively short existence up until 1859 when it merged with and was subsumed into a company by the name of the Lancashire and Yorkshire Railway (L&YR), a longstanding rival as evidenced by the so-called '*Clifton Blockade*' of 1849.

The existence of Ramsbottom as a railway town continued long after 1859. During this period, the advent of railways offered unprecedented speed and affordability of travel and was not only a boon to industrialists but also opened up new horizons for passengers.

The townsfolk of Ramsbottom and other neighbouring areas benefitted greatly from the enhanced leisure opportunities that arose. A theme that recurs very often in first-hand accounts is of trips to the seaside and to attractions such as Belle Vue Pleasure Gardens in Manchester. During these earlier days of rail, there were also unfortunately a lot of accidents on track. With such steep gradients operating in East Lancashire, stories abound of 'runaway trains'.

It is not easy to pinpoint a particular period which could be identified as marking the heyday of railways. However, in terms of steam locomotives, the 20th century inter-war period evokes a time when *Flying Scotsman* and *Mallard* were at the height of their powers, not only breaking speed records but creating enduring images in the minds of those who were fortunate either to travel on them or witness their majestic motion from the trackside. The special connection the *Scotsman* has had with the ELR and Ramsbottom, over the last 30 years, is explored in these pages.

The sad story is also told of how the writing was on the wall, from the late 1950s onwards, for the survival chances of the rail system as it then was. Years of neglect, with the government becoming much more inclined to invest in new roadways based on rapidly increasing car use, brought about a crisis concerning the viability of railways. The crunch was set to come in the early 1960's with the so-called *'Beeching Cuts'* which had such a devastating effect on the national rail network as a whole.

With Ramsbottom and East Lancashire drastically affected, proposed closure of many local lines aroused strong adverse community reaction. Nowhere were protests fiercer than in neighbouring Summerseat where law-breaking demonstrations in 1968 led to police arrests. By the end of the decade though, government decisions came into force and the railway identity of towns such as Ramsbottom seemed doomed irrevocably.

The closure and subsequent demolition of Ramsbottom railway station in 1972 at the time signified the end of an era in the town's history going back to 1846. The local press reported the station falling prey to 'souvenir hunters' combing the site for relic items such as old tickets stashed away in cupboards.

Remarkably, a brave rearguard campaign sprang up from 1966 onwards amongst a small group of activists based at first in Helmshore. When it had become obvious though that there was no chance of keeping the track open there, the group, calling itself the East Lancashire Railway Preservation Society (ELRPS) transferred its operational headquarters to Bury. The perseverance shown by the ELRPS over many years led finally to the triumphant re-opening of the line between Bury and Ramsbottom in 1987.

It is hard to imagine now, nearly forty years later, the transformation that the return of the railway made to a town

Introduction

which, prior to 1987, bore all the characteristic signs of a run-down ex-cotton centre. This study captures a wide range of views and opinions put forward by people at that time, reflecting not only what it meant to them personally but what the return of the railway was seen to offer to the life of the town as a whole. Playing a key part in the subsequent success of the ELR heritage line, Ramsbottom has developed a major reputation, not only as a tourist attraction but as a fine place to live.

Talking of which, I will bring this introduction to a finish on something of a personal note about the circumstances of coming to live here in Ramsbottom myself. In a strange way, it might not have happened if the original railway station construction had not been knocked down in 1972. What is the connection?

In short, a fortuitous one. John Lawrence, manager of the local paper mill, casting an interested eye on the station's stone-work, negotiated to buy it off British Railways. Supervising its careful dismantling, one stone at a time, the precious raw materials were then transferred to a new location situated a few hundred yards up the road from the bottom of Bridge Street.

Intent at the time on building a new home for himself and his family, John had bought a plot of land on a corner of the road leading at a right angle down to Nuttall Hall Road. This residence was to become known as 42, Bury New Road, built in the 1970s but significant in architectural terms for the fact that it was constructed from the original stone-work of the railway station built in 1846.

I am not saying this 'back-story' played any great part in the decision of my wife Anna and I to buy and move into 42, Bury New Road in 2000, but it certainly sparked our interest to learn about this intriguing aspect of the property. I would like to think that it has also, in an indirect way, played some part in motivating me to write this book!

Nigel Jepson, March 31, 2023

CHAPTER ONE –

Transport in the area before the advent of railways

Road transport
Up to the middle of the 18th century, ancient footpaths had continued to serve a useful purpose as far as transporting goods was concerned. This was mainly because, in the local Ramsbottom area, industry was still largely based on the *'Domestic System'* - a method of work-operation that could cope well enough by means of conveying goods by cart or on horseback.

The earliest detailed map covering the area, *Yates' survey of 1783*, shows in fact that the town of Ramsbottom only amounted to a few scattered houses and had barely yet come into existence. The main settlement in the local area was based at Holcombe with the advantage it had of occupying higher, drier land.

With regard to local road routes, there were two particularly worthy of note. One descended from the moors above Shuttleworth. Dropping down Shipperbottom Lane, it crossed the River Irwell via a ford, running alongside the river at the village of Nuttall before ascending to Holcombe and beyond.

Secondly, there was 'a road through Ramsbottom which followed Crow Lane, swung right up Water Street (latterly called Bridge Street) by Crow Trees Farm and the township Dungeon opposite, up Carr Street, through another right-angle bend by the *Rose and Crown*, up the 1 in 4 incline of the Rake, past Holcombe Chapel, along Cross Lane and down the narrow, often watery Holcombe Old Road, to emerge by the *Hare and Hounds*.'[1]

Ramsbottom experienced its first significant industrial growth with the building of a large mill in 1783 by business-partners Robert Peel and William Yates, creating the Ramsbottom Print Works for their expanding calico and bleaching business on a site later to become known as the 'Old Ground'. Whilst the hilly nature of surrounding terrain helped provide water power, the factory owners encountered difficulties in the early years over the transporting of goods to and from their factory.

Matters improved with the emergence of so-called *turnpike roads* during the course of the second half of the 18th century, a system whereby road-builders were authorised by the government to build higher quality roads, with the right granted to charge tolls to road-users. A turnpike road going through Shuttleworth from Bury to Haslingden (and then linking up with the Blackburn and Whalley turnpike road) had been authorised in 1789. The contractor who was responsible for building about seven miles of road belonging to the Bury, Haslingden, Blackburn and Whalley Trust was a famous road-builder of the time John Metcalf, also known as 'Blind Jack of Knaresborough'. Another such road, which passed through the centre of Ramsbottom, was constructed from Edenfield to Little Bolton in 1797, now the A676.

By 1800, there were four *turnpikes* meeting at Edenfield, bringing opportunities in due course for local people to make a living as carriers. For example, James Whittaker, founding his business in 1825, was to prove the most successful. The coming of the railways was further to add to his fortunes as a carrier of goods.

Robert Peel Senior
Robert Peel Senior's influence cannot be underestimated, not only in terms of providing a platform for the expansion of industry in Ramsbottom but also improving the means of transport available for the purpose of tapping into local markets and further afield. While it was highly convenient for him that the Edenfield to Little Bolton road passed through the centre of town, it was more challenging to link up at the Shuttleworth end.

First, a road (to become known as Peel Brow) had been built and also a bridge over the River Irwell by Peel and Yates

c. 1789, originally called Ramsbottom Bridge and then later Peel Bridge. It connected their calico printing premises at the Old Ground with Peel Brow, the link road up to the Bury and Haslingden turnpike. At the same time, road-users had to stop at the Peel Bridge tollgate to pay a toll to use the road. This latter arrangement was to prove a particular headache in the railway era, compounding traffic congestion at the foot of Bridge Street.

However looking back earlier to the end of the 18th century, such developments provided an enormous stimulus to the growth of local industry, making transporting of goods much easier. An incidental effect of this spate of general road development in the area was that while Ramsbottom developed strongly, the Nuttall settlement was gradually to find itself becoming more isolated as time went on. [2]

Further Industrial Development
From the start of the 19th century onwards, other major factories had sprung up apace in Ramsbottom. In 1802, the Ashtons, brothers James and John, had built Ramsbottom Mill, the town's first big spinning mill, located on Crow Lane. By the mid-1830s, this was to become the biggest mill in the Irwell Valley with three enormous waterwheels and three powerful steam engines. As in the case of Peel and Yates, who also had factories in Bury and Burrs, the Ashtons too owned factories elsewhere, in Middleton and Hyde.

Meanwhile in 1806, 'William Grant and Brothers' had come to acquire Robert Peel's Print Works. From this point onwards, the rise of the Grants had proved meteoric. Not long after in 1812, the firm had gone on to buy Nuttall Mill, together with its surrounding estate, previously owned by a Mr Alsop. At the start of the 1820s, they had decided to re-locate from 'The Old Ground' to 'The Square', a large site surrounded almost on all sides in moat-like fashion by the River Irwell.

It was the Grants and Ashtons - together with the Duckworths (owners of Shipperbottom coalpit, probably on Whitelow Lane) - who were responsible for the building of Bury New Road in the mid-1830s, which was intended to provide a gentler gradient than that of Peel Brow out of Ramsbottom to link up with the Bury to Haslingden road.[3]

There is no doubting the massive influence that the Grant Brothers came to exert in Ramsbottom during these times. As a family that had migrated almost penniless in the 1780s from their Speyside home in the Scottish Highlands, in order to carve out a living for themselves in East Lancashire, they had certainly landed on their feet in Ramsbottom.

After acquiring the Park Estate in 1827, the imposing four-storey Grants Tower - which was to command the landscape until its eventual collapse in the mid-20th century - had been erected the year after in honour of dynastic parents William and Grace, who had died in 1817 and 1821 respectively. This was sited at 'The Top o' th' Hoof' on a hill-top high up above the road where William senior had once significantly paused, towards the end of the family's long trek down from Scotland in 1783, to admire the view down to the Irwell valley, likening it to his beloved Speyside.

A family that always stuck together with clan-like solidarity, it was William Grant (1769-1842) who played the role of senior partner in the quest during these years to accumulate ever-increasing amounts of property in the area, both industrial and landed. His main business partner was Daniel. The two of them were thereafter to be immortalised by their biographer William Hume Elliot fostering a belief that Charles Dickens, in the course of writing his novel *Nicholas Nickleby*, had based his two philanthropic factory-owner characters, the Cheeryble brothers, on William and Daniel Grant.

Away from factory life, these two brothers shared residence at Springside, originally bought in 1815, a mansion lying on the Walmersley Road between Ramsbottom and Bury. Regarding another leading member of the 'Grant clan', it was said that John was 'more of a yeoman than a merchant or manufacturer' and 'admirably managed the landed property acquired by the firm'.[4]

This 'landed property' featured the splendid Nuttall Hall which comprised 20 rooms and had a glazed dome in the roof. Its large imposing hall combined chandeliers and fine tapestries. The mansion was set in two acres of gardens.

Blighted Chances of a Railway Connection to Ramsbottom

As far as trends in transport were concerned, the 1840s were set to become known as the decade of *'Railway Mania'*. The drama surrounding the opening of the Liverpool to Manchester line in 1830 and the amazing feats achieved by Stephenson's *'Rocket'* held out enormous opportunities for other business enterprises to seek to emulate.

Initially, things had looked promising in terms of Ramsbottom gaining a rail connection. As early as 1830 for example, the Manchester, Bolton and Bury Canal Company had sought to promote the construction of a railway along the line of their canal from Salford to Bolton and Bury. An Act of Parliament was passed to enable them to become a railway company and the original plan was to connect up all three centres by rail. However, the line was destined not to go as far as Bury after the company's engineer, Jesse Hartley, decided that the many engineering feats needing to be undertaken, including for example a 1,100 yard tunnel on a gradient of 1 in 100, were too expensive to carry out. In these circumstances, Bury was left out of the equation, at the same time ruling out the possibility of any extension into parts of Rossendale which might naturally have followed on.

The opening of a line between Manchester and Bolton took place on 29 May 1838 but it was to go no further for the time being. At the start of the 1840s, Bury and Rossendale were left isolated and seemingly out on a limb, a situation that was felt most acutely by local businessmen such as the Ashtons and the Grants. At this critical point in time, it was evident that the problem could only be solved by East Lancashire entrepreneurs getting their heads together to sort matters out for themselves.

Notes
1. Andrew Todd, 1987, *An Introduction to Ramsbottom* for ELR
2. *Nuttall – Ramsbottom's Lost Village*, pub. Ramsbottom Heritage Society, p.14
3. Andrew Todd, 1995, *Around Ramsbottom,* pub. Ramsbottom Heritage Society, p.85
4. William Hume Elliot, 1906, *The Story of the "Cheeryble" Grants*, pub. Sherratt and Hughes, p.122

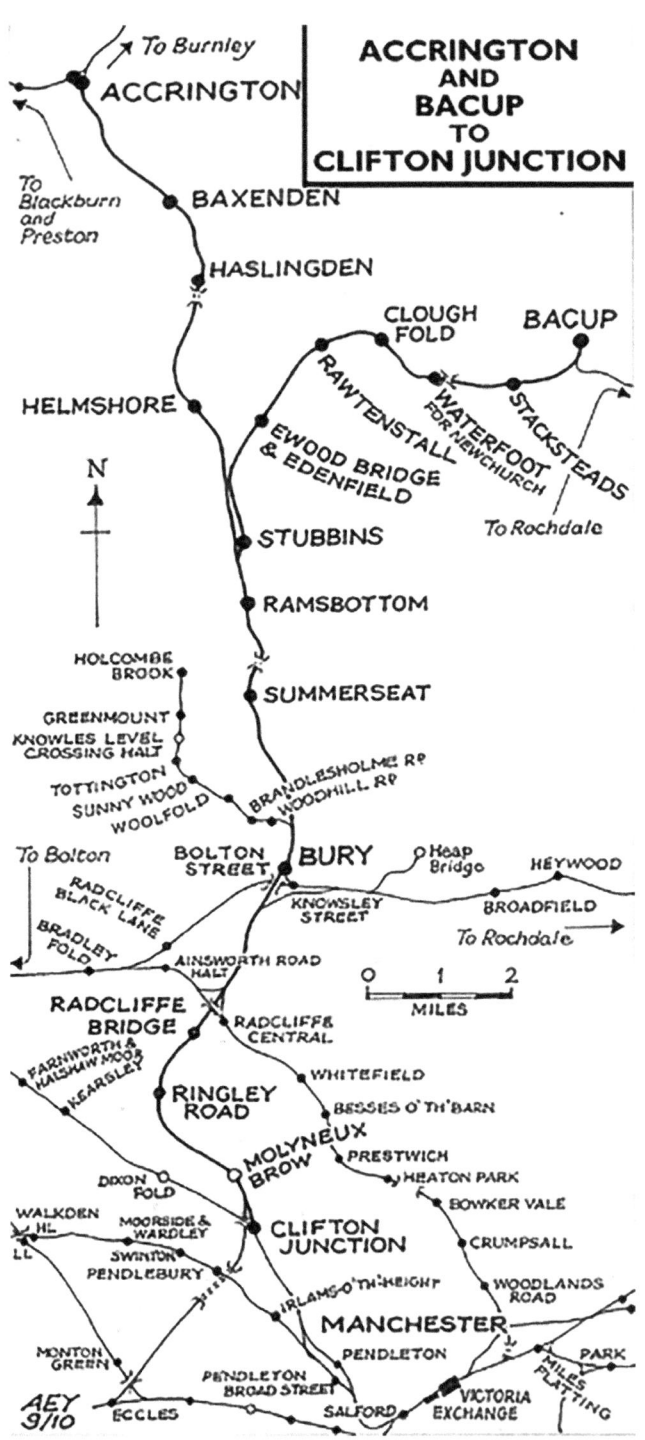

CHAPTER TWO –

'Alarming riot' of rail workers at the *Grant Arms*

Important Meeting at the *Red Lion Inn* in Bury
On 14 September 1843, a highly significant meeting took place when a group of leading East Lancashire businessmen met at the *Red Lion Inn* in Bury to discuss escalating concerns over the lack of a rail connection to the area. By the end of this meeting, it had been decided that the project of building a railway joining Manchester, Bury, Ramsbottom and Rawtenstall was 'worthy of being entertained'. A provisional committee was set up, involving local Ramsbottom mill-owners, the Ashtons, as well as other district businessmen/leaders. These were Thomas Wrigley and John Grundy (two paper manufacturers operating in Heap Bridge, close to Bury), Richard Walker (MP for Bury), John Robinson Kay (Brooksbottoms Mill owner in Summerseat, who also had a mill in Rawtenstall), Henry Hoyle Hardman and David Whitehead (mill-owners in Rawtenstall).

Although there is no record found of any of the Grant Brothers serving on this particular committee, they would no doubt have supported the case for making Ramsbottom an important stop-off point on the envisaged line connecting Bury and Rawtenstall.

Another major project backer was Thomas Aitken, a cotton manufacturer who by this time owned two mills, one in Chatterton, near Stubbins, and the other in Irwell Vale. The former-mentioned site had been the infamous location of the 'Chatterton Riot' of 1826. In that year, an angry mob of workers, despite local Justice of the Peace William Grant having read out the *Riot Act*, went on to smash newly-installed labour-saving machinery at the mill, at that time owned by Thomas' father William Aitken. This incurred a reaction from the assembled military that had led to the death of five people.

Moving forward though to the present point in time, Thomas Aitken set himself to subscribe £2,500 to the railway scheme and become one of the original directors of the soon-to-be-formed company.

Establishment of the Manchester, Bury and Rossendale Railway (MB&RR)

The outcome reached at the meeting at the *Red Lion* was an agreement to set up a company assuming the title of 'The Manchester, Bury and Rossendale Railway (MB&RR)'. A follow-up meeting took place shortly afterwards at the *Eagle and Child Inn* in Bury on 29 September 1843. Richard Walker acted as chairman.

The results of a traffic count were made known to the gathering. From this survey, it was encouragingly noted that '6,000 people travelled by some kind of conveyance along Manchester Road per week and it was estimated that the revenue for rail passengers and goods between Manchester and Rawtenstall would result in a dividend of 10% on the proposed capital of £300,000 (roughly the equivalent of £32 million in modern day terms) to be raised by 12,000 shares, with a value of £25, requiring a deposit of £2.50 per share.'[1]

The initial aim was to construct a double track railway from Clifton, forming a junction with the Manchester and Bolton line. The plan also however opened up the possibility of extending the line northwards from Bury along the Irwell Valley to reach Rawtenstall via Ramsbottom.

Without doubt, it was local industrialists who pulled the strings in the railway development that came about in the area. Planning around the operation was geared pivotally around providing enhanced transport connections to and from factories and mill-sites. This factor also dictated elements of infrastructure such as the siting of stations and sidings en route.

The Formation and Development of the East Lancashire Railway Company

On 4 July 1844, the private bill put forward by the MB&RR was given Royal Assent. The Act authorised the company to raise £300,000 and also granted the right to borrow £100,000.

Throughout this period, it has to be said that the Government never looked to put obstacles in the path of new railway ventures. With minimal regulation, any group of individuals could form a company, seek to gain investment and then submit a bill to Parliament in order to have the right to acquire land for the route of the proposed railway. Since many MPs themselves, like the Bury MP Richard Walker, were investors in such schemes, it was exceedingly rare for Parliament to reject a bill. The trickier part for rail entrepreneurs was translating the bill into profitable practice.

Two surveyors, Thomas Gooch and Charles Cawley were appointed to map out the precise route from Clifton Junction through to Rawtenstall. Thomas Gooch, born in 1808, was from Bedlington, Northumberland and had previously been apprenticed to George Stephenson, the so-called *'Father of Railways'* who had played such a massive role in the creation of the Liverpool to Manchester line in 1830 involving the steam locomotive, *'Rocket'*. Gooch had been Stephenson's assistant in the surveying of the route for the Manchester and Leeds railway. Meanwhile, Charles Cawley was a local East Lancashire man, born at Middleton in 1812.

Following the survey, a plan was devised to build the railway line to run north from Clifton through a cutting at Outwood, requiring the removal of about 600,000 cubic yards (460,000 cubic metres) of earth. From this point, the line would pass north-east through Radcliffe Bridge and then into Bury Bolton Street station. From Bury, it was to pass through Summerseat, Ramsbottom, Stubbins, Ewood Bridge, Irwell Vale and finally on to Rawtenstall. It was appreciated that the railway needed to climb a constant gradient, calling for several engineering feats to be carried out, including a variety of viaducts, tunnels, cuttings and embankments.

Reflecting the frenzied approach to railway-building at the time, preliminary discussions had also been taking place in surrounding districts to the north of Bury and Rossendale, as to other lines being laid. For example a 'Blackburn, Burnley, Accrington & Colne Extension Railway' was seeking to come into existence.

At a meeting on 17 October 1843, a group of landowners, merchants and traders from Accrington had sought to convince the provisional committee of the MB&RR that their undertaking should extend to Accrington via a continuation of the line from Stubbins Junction (situated between Ramsbottom and Rawtenstall) northwards to meet the west-to-east Preston to Burnley route at Accrington.

This proposed further extension was authorised by an Act of Parliament of 30 June 1845. With the two companies seeing eye-to-eye, an amalgamation came about by further Act of Parliament on 24 July 1845, at which point in time the MB&RR absorbed the other company, trading from now on under the heading of the East Lancashire Railway.

Operational Challenges

The contract for constructing the Clifton to Rawtenstall section was awarded in May 1844 to Pauling and Henfrey, a Manchester firm of contractors. This firm had recently become involved in building new barracks on Bolton Road in Bury which the Government had wanted constructed quickly in order to have soldiers stationed in the area to combat widespread Chartist social unrest at this time. If the decade of the 1840s was characterised in one way by *'Railway Mania'*, it was also to be known as the *'Hungry Forties'* with massive poverty and perceived threat to law and order from protest movements such as Chartism. During this time, Chartist leaders like Peter Murray McDouall, a doctor with a practice at 18 Bolton Street in Ramsbottom (present-day *John the Jeweller's*), found the existing northern railway system very useful for attending rallies or else, on occasion, making speedy getaways to avoid arrest. [2]

On 12 August 1844, John Hawkshaw was appointed consulting engineer, a man whose services were much sought after at this time. He did not stay long in post though, resigning in December 1844 due to an existing obligation to support the M&LR extension from Heywood to Bury. In the same year, the position of assistant engineer had been taken up by John Shae Perring, who was to become chief engineer from May 1846 onwards.

Pauling and Henfrey's tender had amounted to £167,529, accepted as two separate contracts, firstly from Clifton to Bury and secondly from Bury to Rawtenstall/Accrington. It was the usual custom for large-scale contractors like Pauling and Henfrey then to sub-let to smaller contractors who undertook to carry out different sections of the work. For example, projects were sub-let to John Kellett at Radcliffe and John Heywood at Nuttall Tunnel, close to Ramsbottom.

Despite separate elements being sub-let, it was appreciated from the start that the success of the scheme depended on all the different elements coming together. Work carried out in the Ramsbottom area, for example, was only as good as the work carried out across the line as a whole.

The hilly nature of the terrain posed major challenges. For example at Clifton, the line had to cross the Irwell valley on a viaduct of thirteen arches, including one of 96 feet (28.8m) span with a height of 80 feet (24m) over the river. Near Radcliffe, the Irwell had to be re-crossed at a height of 70 feet (21m) on a wooden viaduct on stone piers, with five spans of 55 feet (16.5m). A mile short of Bury, the river was crossed for the third time by an iron bridge of 100 feet-span (30m).

Translating plans into action went anything but smoothly. The first problem during the summer of 1845 was a workers' recruitment crisis. Given the amount of railway lines that were being built up and down the country at this time, it was perhaps no real surprise there was a shortage. Measures were taken to try and address the shortfall but these sometimes could be counter-productive. For example, seven men who had complied with an arrangement to work Sundays had ended up being charged with the offence of breaking the Sabbath. [3]

The winter of 1845/6 saw continuous wet weather which made levelling up land most challenging. Landslips occurred and efforts to build embankments were washed away as quickly as they had been mounted up. However, by the start of 1846, the recruitment crisis had eased and before long 700 'navvies' (a term borrowed from the 'navigator' work-force that had built the canals) were engaged working on the line between Bury and Rawtenstall.

It was far from plain sailing for employers though with troubles flaring up at times between different sections of the work-force. With only a skeleton police-force on the ground at the time, help call-outs had to be made to Bury. For example, in May 1846, an episode occurred in which: 'an alarming riot took place among the labourers on the East Lancashire Railway at Ramsbottom. Disturbances arose from a dispute respecting wages between two English and two Irish labourers (in the *Grant Arms*) who succeeded in enlisting the backing of their respective countrymen into the quarrels and nearly 2,000 men were at one time engaged…Many men on both sides were severely beaten and a number of Irish were driven from their homes…previously to the arrival from Bury of the police under Inspector McDonald who succeeded in dispersing the riot. The police remained on duty all night and yesterday all was perfectly quiet.' [4]

The occasion of monthly pay-outs often led to serious disturbances when, with money in their pockets, the 'navvies' went out on an extended 'randy'. Without question, these men habitually worked hard but when the opportunity came to carouse, they drank and played even harder. In a telling description of their general attitude to life, it was said that 'they were heathens, in the heart of Christian people, savages in the midst of civilisation and it is scarcely an exaggeration to say, that a feeling something akin to that which awed the Roman when the Goth was at his gates, opened up in the minds of those citizens near where the railway labourer pitched his tent…They lived only for the present; they cared not for the past and were indifferent to the future.' [5]

Difficulties of a different nature arose when chief contractors Pauling and Henfrey were charged with misleading the Company about how much time was needed to construct the line. With progress slipping behind schedule, Pauling and Henfrey ended up being sacked from the job and the contract given to John Waring instead. This firm had stronger experience of building railways, for example for the York and North Midland. To add insult to injury as far as the dismissed Manchester firm was concerned, much of their equipment was seized off them by way of extracting compensation.

Process of Land Purchase
Looking on the more positive side, the ELR had experienced relatively few problems to date in purchasing the land it required. Tithe surveys of the time confirmed that much of the land along the projected route was made up of 'waste, woodland, pasture or reservoirs, except at Brooksbottom (described locally as *'Brox'*) where arable land was avoided by the tunnel'. [6]

The chief landowner along the route was the Earl of Derby. Recognising he was in a strong bargaining position, he quickly appreciated there were healthy profits to be gained from the fact that the ELR needed to buy land off him. Naturally, his chief steward bargained for the highest price he could on behalf of his master. In comparison with other sellers, the Earl capitalised on his exalted status by levying a sum of £400 per acre for his land whereas the going rate generally appeared to be about half this amount per acre for those with lesser bargaining power.

Response of local landowners in the Ramsbottom area
Others figures such as John Robinson Kay had influential roles to play. Although appreciating the obvious economic benefit that rail connection brought to his business interests, Kay was also mindful of safeguarding the land properties he owned in the area.

Tracing Kay's family background, his father Thomas Kay, owner of Longholme Mills, Rawtenstall, had in 1829 bought him Brooksbottoms Mill (built in 1773) in Summerseat from Richard Hamer whose daughter Mary became Kay's wife in 1834, also to bring him Wood Road Mill on her father's death in 1850. With railway development underway in the local area, Kay was naturally keen to reap the benefits of the connection.

The section of line from Summerseat Station onwards proved very challenging, for one thing necessitating building a 400-yard (360m) long viaduct. A further short distance along the same line, a 423-yard (380m) tunnel also looked as it would have to be bored through solid rock in order to enable ELR trains to progress towards the next station at Ramsbottom.

At the time, Kay might well have had concerns that his handsome residential property, Walmersley House, situated on the road between Ramsbottom and Bury, could conceivably get caught up in the planning web. Having much to gain from the railway connection in one sense, Kay also potentially had a lot to lose if the ELR route-plan worked against him in other ways. With a strong interest in the direction in which rail transport developed in the local area, he had worked towards becoming a Director of the East Lancashire Railway. In the event, both his business premises and residential properties were to remain unscathed.

The Grants fight stubborn rearguard action

In accordance with the ELR's stated intention of 'not wishing to inflame the good will of the mill owners', the devised route in relation to Ramsbottom (including sidings provision) duly connected up with but did not otherwise impinge on the Square Works, nor other important industrial premises in the town such as the Ashtons' Ramsbottom Mill. While the ELR seemed happy enough to leave the industrial premises of the town's leading mill-owners wholly intact, a dilemma emerged though with regard to the Grant Brothers' private properties in the area. First, there was Daniel's Springside Hall residence - elder brother William had died in 1842 - situated between Bury and Ramsbottom to take into account.

Then there was Nuttall Hall, standing close to the Square Works on the other side of the banks of the River Irwell. Set in two acres of gardens, with woodland walks, ponds and waterfalls, all these features were designed to add to the idyllic, peaceful aura of the location. Occupying the palatial Nuttall Hall with wife Elizabeth and children, John Grant also had responsibility for the working operation of Nuttall Mill and the Hall Farm.

Extensive landowners to the north of Bury, the Grants were also major shareholders in the railway company. Tensions surfaced when the ELR announced that its route from Bury to

Ramsbottom ran across edges of both Springside and Nuttall estates.

Daniel Grant, for his part, became embroiled in a long-running dispute with the ELR 'Land Committee', the body bearing responsibility for having to resolve difficulties arising out of such issues. A series of negotiations ensued which had started with Daniel submitting a compensation claim for £5,000 on mere account of the line being visible from his land. In response, the ELR Land Committee at first only offered £2,000, which Daniel dismissed as paltry. The amount offered was raised to £4,000 but not accepted. In the end, compromise was reached with Daniel settling for compensation at a rate which did not come cheaply for the company at £4,500 (the equivalent of over £500,000 in today's values).

Likewise, John Grant was far from happy about the extent to which the line's route affected the tranquillity of his Nuttall Hall estate. 'Not in my back yard' was his approach to the prospect of railway commotion despoiling the peace and serenity of his grounds. On this basis, the ELR was obliged at John's insistence to undertake the building of the 115-yard (106m) Nuttall Tunnel, appeasing the squire's demand that his cherished view of the River Irwell should remain unsullied.

Furthermore, John was fastidious with regard to how the tunnel should look, demanding that it be castellated in a manner consistent with the architectural style of Nuttall Hall Farm. Certain distinctive features were incorporated into the tunnel's north entrance, including a coat of arms, a Lancashire rose, capped by a frieze decorated with seven carved, rather ghoulish-looking faces. This subsequently gave rise to speculation as to whether the faces were meant to represent those of directors of the East Lancashire Railway Company.

Notes
1. Minutes of Meeting of the Provisional Committee of the MB&BR, 29 September 1843
2. Nigel Jepson, 2021, *Ramsbottom's Revolutionary Doctor*, pub. YouCaxton, p. 97
3. *Manchester Guardian*, 26 September 1845

4. *Manchester Guardian*, 20 May 1846
5. John Francis, 1851, *History of the English Railway, 1820-1845 Vol II*, p.69
6. Jeffrey Wells, 1995, *Railways In And Around Bury*, pub. Challenger, p.3

CHAPTER THREE -

Ramsbottom becomes Railway Town in 1846

Approval given and invitations sent out

Events took a very positive turn when it was announced that the 14-mile stretch of line between Clifton and Rawtenstall was ready to be surveyed on behalf of the Board of Trade. The process was carried out by the national Inspector-General of Railways, Sir Charles Pasley. Following his inspection on 23 September 1846, Pasley gave the final go-ahead for the service to commence operation. He was reported to have been 'very highly pleased with the good substantial character of the works'. [1]

Since the original meeting of Bury and Rossendale businessmen at the *Red Lion*, it seemed a remarkably short space of time of three years before the project had been completed and come into operation. The advent of the railway was undoubtedly set to transform lives and livelihoods within the Bury and Rossendale business communities that had fought so hard to create a local rail network.

Meanwhile, upwards of 1,000 invitations had already been sent out to company officials, shareholders and other local citizens in anticipation of the first journey along the line set to take place on Friday 25 September, only two days after Pasley's official authorisation. The conventional procedure was to run a celebratory 'special service' before the line was opened to the broader public. So it was that many of the invited guests gathered at Manchester Victoria station on Hunt's Bank on the Friday. *Bradshaw's Railway Gazette (1846)* remarked upon a distinguished number of people waiting on the platform including for example 'C. Nicholson, Esq, mayor of Kendal, managing director of the East Lancashire Railway'.[2]

From those who had been present at that inaugural meeting held at the *Red Lion* in September 1843, various Ashton family members, representing the interests of Ramsbottom Mill, were reported as present alongside other notable local entrepreneurs such as John Robinson Kay, Thomas Aitken, Thomas Wrigley and John Grundy – who had become chairman of the board of directors by this time. No doubt those manufacturers hailing from Rawtenstall – such as Henry Hoyle Hardman and David Whitehead – made an appearance at a point further down the line.

'…The train left Victoria station at twenty minutes past twelve o'clock, consisting of twenty carriages, drawn by the new and powerful steam-engine the *'Irwell'*, which was profusely decorated with small flags'.

A second locomotive was attached at Clifton Junction, at which stage the train ran onto the East Lancashire Railway itself. This was the point at which, as described earlier, several engineering feats had had to be carried out. For example, Clifton Viaduct, consisting of thirteen stone arches, carried the line over the Irwell Valley.

Arriving in Bury at 1.15, the train service had the honour of being the first ever to enter the town. Halting there, the services of a third engine were enlisted and a further batch of coaches added. The experience of arriving in Bury was far from edifying in other ways though. Passengers found themselves in the middle of a huge building-site given that Bolton Street station was still in the throes of construction. However, this did nothing to dampen the spirits of rail-goers caught up in the excitement of participating in the opening of this long-awaited stretch of new railway.

Inaugural train heading towards Ramsbottom
From Bury onwards, the number of coach carriages, painted sky blue and bearing the company's coat of arms, had grown to thirty-three in total. Lifting the atmosphere further, the 5th Regiment of

Foot military band played popular tunes of the day for the benefit of the distinguished ensemble of passengers.

Just beyond Summerseat station, the train was carried over the River Irwell by a 400-yard long viaduct of eleven arches adjacent to the works of John Robinson Kay before disappearing in quick succession into the Brooksbottom and Nuttall tunnels. Emerging back out into daylight, passengers would have quickly caught sight of the four-storey Grants Tower.

Crossing the Irwell again, this time over a trussed timber bridge, the line was carried over reservoirs by a viaduct of iron girders on stone piers before arriving, four miles down the line from Bury, at Ramsbottom with a sight of the Grant Brothers' Square Works to the left of the line.

From this point as far as Stubbins Bridge, the line was borne on a mile-long embankment before tackling the last more level stretch of the outward journey. With a palpable air of celebration, the special train eventually reached Rawtenstall station having taken thirty minutes to get there from Bury.

'Shortly after the arrival of the train, about five hundred ladies and gentlemen sat down to a sumptuous collation in one of the immense power-loom sheds in the works of J. Robinson Kay, Esq. John Grundy Esq. presided and J. Robinson Kay, Esq. occupied the vice-chair'.[3]

Guests listened to several celebratory speeches, including one from managing director Cornelius Nicholson. A relative stranger to Bury and Rossendale, the ex-Mayor of Kendal had one thing in common though with the community – he was a paper maker. In terms of an existing railway connection, Cornelius had been closely associated with the Lancashire & Carlisle and the Kendal & Windermere railways in their early days. Irrespective of anything else, he chose 'on this occasion to launch into a learned discourse on the Forest of Rossendale, which lasted for the best part of an hour.'[4]

Three days later, on Monday 28 September 1846, the railway service opened to the public with a schedule of fourteen trains running daily between Salford and Bury in each direction, five of these reaching Ramsbottom and going on to Rawtenstall. Five trains travelled on Sundays. Facilities for goods traffic were to become available for use in 1847.

Effects on Ramsbottom from the advent of rail transport
Being linked up by rail was undoubtedly of enormous benefit to the town. The level of industry that had grown up in the years before the advent of railway was such that this new form of transport was both a boon to existing businesses and a spur to further development of the town.

Trying to gain an idea of the scale of increasing population, there was a census in 1841 but it provides only limited information about the Ramsbottom area. The fuller census of 1851 gives a total of 2,224, which was set to rise to 4,205 by 1881. In industrial terms, whereas during the 1840s, there had been five mills trading in cotton or wool, the number had risen to fourteen by the start of the 1880s. In addition, new industries had sprung up, including engineering, paper and soap works. This growth was in no small part due to the coming of the railway which, as well as encouraging additional industry to the town, also brought a change in the direction of new building development, concentrating increasingly on the area surrounding Bridge Street or what might be called 'Lower Ramsbottom'.

Before the coming of the railway, the terrain around where the station was built had largely been meadow land on the banks of the River Irwell. Given the growth in the number of new factory sites springing up in recent times in close proximity to the railway line, urgent consideration had to be given to providing living accommodation for an ever-expanding industrial work-force. For example, terraces of workers' cottages were soon being erected on sites behind St. Paul's Church. For certain, the town's fulcrum moved ever more strongly southwards drawn by the magnet of the railway connection.

The entrepreneurial spirit of leading industrialists played a key part in the development of the town during these pivotal years. From the first quarter of the 19th century onwards, as well as the Ashtons at Ramsbottom Mill, the Grant Brothers provided an inspiring example of how local businessmen had managed to prove so successful in promoting the industrial interests of the town. The Grants' Square Works, opened in 1821, had prospered for many years to date. Even so, the enterprise clearly stood to prosper further from the advent of railways, especially given a close trackside location. It hadn't been long before a siding agreement had been established which was specifically geared towards meeting the transport needs of the Square Works.

To put into context the overall savings to be made by local businesses from the coming of the railway, the cost of transporting goods between Manchester and Rawtenstall by road in 1844 had been £1 and ½ pence per ton per mile. In contrast, the maximum charges laid down under the new railway's tariffs were 'for road stone and agricultural materials 2d. per ton per mile, foodstuffs 3½d per ton per mile and for raw materials and manufactured goods 4d per ton per mile.' [5]

Enhanced speed of transport was also a vitally important element in the process of what the railway had to offer. For example, the existing 2½ hour length of time for a passenger road journey between Manchester and Rawtenstall was set to be reduced to less than an hour by rail. As far as Ramsbottom was concerned, it meant that a train leaving Bury at 7.50 am would arrive at 8.08 and thence on to Rawtenstall for 8.20.

By way of knock-on effect, rapid rail development undoubtedly had severe adverse repercussions on road transport. For example, the income of the Bury, Haslingden and Whalley turnpike, standing at £11,264 in 1845, fell to £8,283 in 1848, further plummeting to £4,892 by 1851. [6]

Ramsbottom station

The ELR stations that were built during these times tended to emerge from one of three general 'models'. Bury Bolton Street, the principal station, was designed to very high specifications by the Manchester-based firm of architects Messrs. Holden.

Most other stations on ELR lines were based on a more modest template, designed by the company's engineer, John Shae Perring. Taking up his post with the ELR in the mid-1840s, whilst still only in his early 30s, Perring had a somewhat unusual career to date, his engineering skills having been employed in excavating Egyptian pyramids during the late 1830s, subsequently recording his findings in the three-volume '*The Pyramids of Gizeh*', published between 1839 and 1842. Rather less monumental in scope than pyramids, Perring's ELR stations, as at Ramsbottom, emerged in a rather more prosaic style of conception, built in stone and consisting of a station-master's room with an adjoining seated waiting area, ladies room and a booking office.

The third and cheapest design adopted the same general principles as above, only using brick and timber as materials. Other even more modest provision had though sprung up in the meantime. Summerseat for example, the next station down the line from Bury, had already been opened by the ELR on 25 June 1846. Not that its facilities could be described as anything but basic, being categorised in the ELR Guide of 1849 as 'a roadside halt'. A driveway led up to the station building – 'consisting of no more than a wooden hut perched on the ground and a small goods yard comprising three sidings, a large goods shed and a 1.5 ton crane.'[7]

Ramsbottom station, opened on 25 September 1846, very much conformed to the standard Perring-style design. Double-track, its two platforms stood south of a level crossing at the bottom of Bridge Street. The main station building stood west of the line on the northbound platform. A stone-built goods shed was also put up west of the line.

On either side of the station were sidings. On the Down side (called so because the line was heading this way from ELR headquarters at Bury) was a stone goods shed which adjoined the platform plus a signal box built on the goods shed wall, known as 'Warehouse Cabin'. On the Up side were sidings which served Ramsbottom Paper Mill and a small engine shed with a single road just north of the level crossing.

Already providing an important link-point between Bury and Rawtenstall, Ramsbottom station was destined to develop even greater strategic significance with the later building of an ELR Extension line to Accrington from 1848 onwards. This line extension would require passengers travelling in that direction to have to change train at Ramsbottom, effectively removing Stubbins from the equation. This was because Stubbins station (opened in January 1847) only had platform capacity to enable it to serve the through line to Rawtenstall. For some time thereafter, the station at Ramsbottom would come to be described on timetables as 'Ramsbottom Junction'.

Railway Hotel, Bridge Street

Across the road from the railway station, a hotel was built in 1848 at 2, Bridge Street, to accommodate the greater number of visitors coming to town on the back of Ramsbottom having become a railway town two years earlier. Little is known about the hotel in its early days except for the fact that *Heap's Directory* of 1850 makes mention of a certain Thomas Knowles. More is learnt about him and those residing on premises from the 1861 census which contains the following information: '*Railway Hotel*, Thomas Knowles (46) Victualler, born in Bolton, Lancashire. His wife Jane Knowles (52) born in Bury, Lancashire. Stepsons, John Booth (23) Engraver and Abel Booth (17) Student, both born in Bury, Lancashire. Jane Nuttall (22) General Servant, born in Bury Lancashire. Ellen Tate (29) General Servant, born in Oldham, Lancashire. The later 1881 census notes that No. 10 Bridge Street had also become part of the *Railway Hotel*.

Opening of stations at Ewood Bridge and Rawtenstall

An intermediate stop-off station, between Stubbins and Rawtenstall, was opened at Ewood Bridge on 28 September 1846. It took its name from the village standing on the Edenfield to Haslingden Turnpike Road where the latter crossed the Irwell. The likeliest reason for establishing a rail station here was to provide interchange between the railway and road coaches plying between Accrington, Blackburn, Clitheroe and Whalley and towns to the south. This coach service was to be discontinued after the establishment of the ELR Accrington line in 1848.

Rawtenstall station, in common with Ramsbottom and Ewood Bridge, had opened on 28 September 1846. It originally served as the single-line terminus for the Manchester-Bury-Rawtenstall line. The station was envisaged as a grander affair enjoying the distinction, in common with Bolton Street Bury, of having been designed by Manchester-based architects Messrs. Holden. Most of its facilities were located on the Up line of the station, consisting of one-storey stone-walled and slate-roofed buildings including waiting rooms, goods offices, inspector's office and the station master's house. However, the ELR plan had always been to continue the line on to Bacup. Following an Act of Parliament passed on 27 July 1846, authorising the extension, it was inevitable that further work would need to be carried out to enhance facilities at Rawtenstall.

As well as now having an authorised plan in hand to work on extending the Bury-Rawtenstall line to Bacup, an Act of Parliament had been passed on 3 August 1846 to build an ELR Extension Line to Accrington, entailing further development for Ramsbottom as a railway town. A single line reached Newchurch in 1848 but it took until 1852 for the follow-up connection to Bacup to be completed.

Early Signalling Arrangements at Ramsbottom
From 1851 census returns, it is interesting to note that two local people were identified as 'appearing to have discharged what we would now consider the signalman's function' at Ramsbottom station. These two ELR employees were '17 year old Robert Hopkinson, living at Factory Bottom, who was enumerated as 'Rail Porter, Signalman' whilst James Sutcliffe, living on Ramsbottom Lane and aged 30, was described as a 'Railway Pointsman'. [8]

Interestingly though, a *Bury Times* report of 31 January 1857 highlighted the fact that any such rudimentary signalman's duties were only carried out during the day. By contrast, it appears that 'nocturnal road users were expected to operate the gates themselves'.

It was under such circumstances that it was reported that 'local grocer Ebenezer Alston successfully sued the ELR for £50, the value of his horse and cart when 'his equipage had been run into by a pilot engine whilst passing the level crossing at Ramsbottom station, between the hours of two and three o'clock on the morning of the 2nd December last, no person being in charge of the gate at the time'. [9]

Whilst there is no certainty as to when Ramsbottom started being manned round the clock, it is clear that, as passenger traffic grew in volume, goods trains had increasingly to run at night with movements into sidings adding to the need for the presence of a signalman. This appeared to do little though to stop the volume of complaints made by road-users about delays and other disservices caused by passing trains.

The ELR had shown itself responsive to such complaints by constructing a footbridge in 1859 over the line to the north of the crossing, round the west and north walls of the signal box. However, this footbridge was not to be without its own perils to users. One James Morris was reported as having died from concussion after a severe fall occurring at 11pm one Saturday evening. Significantly, a coroner's inquest, held at the nearby *Railway Hotel*, ruled out any suggestion that Morris might have been worse for wear from excessive drinking after Morris' widow had testified that 'he had left home that evening with three shillings, and there was still two shillings seven and a half pence on his person when he had met his death'.

By way of further telling detail, the keeper of the nearby tollhouse had declared at the same inquest 'that since the bridge had been erected, just two months before, a man, woman and several children had fallen'. [10]

Congestion issues raised in Parliament
From the late 1840s onwards, the station was not only used extensively for commercial purposes by textile manufacturers such as the Grants and Ashtons but by a host of local traders covering a wide range of other business interests. For example, with 'the absence of refrigeration before the 1880s necessitating daily deliverables of perishable food – local butchers collected their meat from the sidings, whilst fish were delivered from Fleetwood or Grimsby'.

There was no doubt that the coming of the railway to Ramsbottom considerably added to options available to the consumer market in terms of increased access to fresh commodities. Benefits accrued in other ways. For example, it made good business for local road conveyance companies: 'Cabs were a constant, as late as the 1920s, horse-drawn hansoms run by Abraham Duckworth (known colloquially as '*Old Ab's Cabs*') queued up outside the station plying for hire'. [11]

Traffic congestion in and around the station area was to create a local nightmare throughout the second half of the 19th century. The Peel Bridge tollgate, located as it was just a few yards to the east, further exacerbated matters. By way of seeking a solution to the problems arising from congestion, the Ramsbottom Local Board had as early as 1867 been petitioning for a road bridge to offset the delays arising from this 'source of great danger, annoyance and inconvenience'. [12]

Although nothing came as a result of the petitioning, discontent had rumbled on through following decades. Moving forward to 1890, the continuing call for a road bridge was highlighted in the local press as follows: 'it is no uncommon thing to see a good half a dozen carts, lorries and carriages wait a good 15 minutes before they can cross the line…Local people are unanimous in their desire to see Ramsbottom station spanned by a bridge, one that will accommodate vehicular as well as pedestrian traffic'. [13]

Three years later, the road bridge idea had been converted into one of building a subway. This new proposal appeared to generate a head of steam. For example, added to all the various local representations, the vexatious issue of the inadequacies of the crossing at Ramsbottom was actually the subject of a parliamentary question put forward by the local MP to the President of the Board of Trade in the House of Commons in 1893. Evidence was cited that 'on 30 September 1893 – 8,948 persons and 181 trains and engines had used the crossing'. [14]

The matter being raised in Parliament might have succeeded in giving added publicity to the issue in hand but was to have no further practical use or outcome. In the end, the subway could only have come into effect if the Local Board had itself been willing to spend ratepayers' money on the scheme but this was not about to happen with road congestion remaining a serious issue for many years to come.

The Peel Bridge tollgate went on operating until 1900. After acquiring Peel's Print Works nearly a century earlier, the Grants and their successors had maintained the right to charge tolls on vehicle traffic. These rights, worth around £145 per annum by

1895, were bought out by the Urban District Council, with tolls being charged for the last time in October 1900.

One particular photograph, taken on the exact day of closure on Friday 26 October 1900, provides evidence of what the tollgate looked like before it was taken 'out of trust' and removed. Incidentally, this same photo represents the earliest pictorial evidence of Ramsbottom's level crossing, its white gates just about visible beyond the Peel Bridge tollgate. Also of interest, showing up in the middle ground, is sight of the hefty footbridge, signals mounted on its roof, and the tiny 1875 stone signal box.

Notes
1. *Manchester Guardian,* 26 September 1846
2. *Bradshaw's Railway Gazette,* September 1846
3. As for Item 2
4. Barry Worthington article in *Bury Times' Rail Commemorative Special,* 24 July 1987
5. MB&BR Act of 1844, pp. 105-6
6. Turnpike Statement and Accounts 1/26, 1848
7. Harrison and Sale's *Guide to the East Lancashire Railway,* 1849
8. Andrew Todd article in Winter 2019 ELR News Magazine: *Memories of Ramsbottom Signalbox and Crossing*s, pp. 16-24
9. *Bury Times,* 31 January 1867
10. *Bury Times,* 26 November 1859
11. As for Item 8 above, p.19
12. *Bury Times,* 31 August 1867
13. *Ramsbottom Observer,* 13 June 1890
14. *Bury Times,* 25 November 1893

CHAPTER FOUR –

Runaway trains and company rivalry

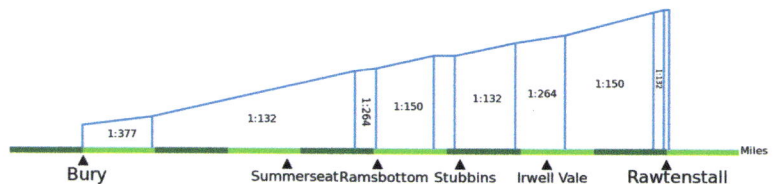

'Leaping out – the only hope!'

Owing to steep gradients on the ELR line from Bury up to Rawtenstall, it was not uncommon for Ramsbottom to be affected by 'runaway trains' during these times when relatively little attention was paid to track safety. One documented example of such an occurrence took place on 28 December 1857:

'when a number of wagons laden with stone broke away from a train in Grane Road sidings, near Haslingden, and ran back down the incline towards Stubbins Junction three miles away. The guard, who had neglected to place pieces of timber between the spokes, jumped aboard the retreating wagons, but fell off near Helmshore Station.'

Catch points were not then in use; nor could anything be done to warn the driver of an oncoming passenger train of the runaway's approach. So violent was the collision that the last two carriages were uncoupled and began to move backwards. In one carriage were Mr. Henry Hargreaves and his sister from Blackburn; in the other was a Mr. Littlewood.

Both men opened a door and as the *Blackburn Standard* was to put it, 'Mr. Hargreaves asked Mr. Littlewood's opinion as to what was best to be done in the hope of effecting their escape. Mr. Littlewood shouted back that leaping out was their only hope. With the carriages rapidly gaining speed, Mr. Hargreaves took this advice and landed on the embankment, knocking himself out, but breaking no bones. Seeing her brother lying motionless by the track, Miss Hargreaves felt unable to follow. Mr. Littlewood also hesitated and it was not until the carriages had shot through Ramsbottom that he flung himself out and was seriously hurt. Miss Hargreaves, in the words of a subsequent newspaper report, 'was hurried on through tunnels until the impetus was exhausted, which was not before the carriages had nearly reached Bury'.

The station master at Ramsbottom, 'who had seen the rapid transit of the carriages past his station, forthwith pursued them with a pilot engine and found Miss Hargreaves pacing backwards and forwards on the line near to a sawmill. He accommodated her with a seat on the tender and provided her with a covering as a protection from the rain, which was then copiously descending. Being thus made safe, she was conveyed on the tender back to Ramsbottom, where she found her brother anxiously awaiting her.'[1]

Given the chaotic nature of events as unfolded that day, it was very lucky that no greater misfortune was suffered. This was not always the case though, as the story of a fatal loss of control on the track in 1860, told later in this chapter, was to demonstrate.

'Clifton Blockade'

The railway era had been characterised from the start by an intense spirit of competition between rival companies. The company which the ELR had most difficulty contending with was the Lancashire and Yorkshire Railway (L&YR). Most notably, on Monday 12 March 1849, a major dispute had broken out between these two companies at Clifton Junction, marking the point at which one company's line started and the other's finished. While an arrangement was in place whereby the ELR paid a sum to the L&YR, based on numbers of passengers, in order for their trains to travel beyond Clifton Junction to Manchester Victoria, the whole practice was very much dependent on mutual trust.

The *Clifton Blockade* happened when the L&YR took a decision to oversee the arrangement more directly, announcing that from 12 March 1849 onwards, trains would actually have to stop at Clifton Junction to allow L&YR officials to board trains to count precise numbers of passengers for themselves.

On the first day of application of the new practice, confrontation took place. To ensure the train stopped at Clifton Junction, the L&YR had resorted to blocking the line with hefty blocks of timber. Meanwhile, the ELR had opposed L&YR officials' efforts to control the logistics of passenger 'transfer' by taking tickets off passengers before that point in the journey was reached. Those suffering most on the day were the passengers themselves who were left facing lengthy delays before reaching their intended destination. A police presence helped resolve matters but the incident was regarded as serious enough, particularly bearing in mind the considerable inconvenience suffered by passengers, as to warrant being raised in the House of Commons on 17 March 1849.

The 'original' ELR closes down in 1859

By the late 1850s, rivalry between the two companies had become rather less intense. In fact, discussions had started to take place regarding a possible amalgamation. Final terms were agreed by the start of 1859. Although amounting largely to a pooling of resources, the deal in effect brought the 15-year-long existence of the ELR to an end, subsumed as it now was under the banner of the L&YR.

In core business terms, the ELR had never been in a strong enough position to compete against other larger companies. During the 1850s, the ELR had in relative terms struggled with the revenue taken for example by such as the L&YR and the London and North West Railway (LNWR), standing at respectively 5 and 15 times more than that by the ELR. [2]

However, it is doubtful whether the switch-over to the L&YR had that much operational effect on stations such as Ramsbottom. For example, under the terms of the 'merger', the ex-ELR headquarters at Bury still remained in active use.

Whilst the L&YR's own locomotive works were sited at Miles Platting in Manchester, the ELR's base at Buckley Wells in Bury continued as before, with the L&YR being prepared to maintain a separate numbering system for the locomotives housed there that were classified as the 'East Lancashire' section.

Railway excursions become ever more popular

The excursion trade was destined to become an ever more popular attraction to the broader public during the 1850s, for example with the running of chartered trips to cities such as Liverpool and seaside resorts like Blackpool and Southport.

It appeared that companies were willing to take on any venture so long as it succeeded in filling carriages. At the more highbrow end of the market, the experience was offered to music-lovers to hear world-renowned soprano Jenny Lind (known as the '*Swedish Nightingale*') perform at the *Theatre Hall Manchester*. On a rather more gruesome note, an option regularly attracting passengers in their thousands was to witness public executions at *Kirkdale Gaol* near Liverpool.

Although the practice of a full week's holiday – known as *Wakes Weeks* – wasn't to come into general use until much later, local firms gradually started to become a little more liberal in granting time for workers to take advantage of day-long rail excursions. However, despite the novelty and excitement involved in such trips, they were not light undertakings in terms of the hardiness required of the traveller. Even as late as 1891, 'a party of excursionists left Ramsbottom for North Wales at 2.00 am on Friday 22 May and arrived back at 5.00 am on Saturday 23 May.' [3]

Unveiling of the Peel Monument: 1852

An example of an excursion that featured Ramsbottom station as a destination was one organised for 8 September 1852. This was to mark the opening of the Peel Monument on top of Holcombe Hill, near Ramsbottom.

Sir Robert Peel (Prime Minister in 1834/5 and again from 1841 to 1846) had been the eldest of eleven children of father Robert Peel, multiple factory-owner, and wife Ellen who was the daughter of Peel's business partner William Yates. The ex-Prime Minister had been born in 1788 at his parents' mansion in the Bury area, Chamber Hall, which incidentally was visible during the late 1840s onwards to passengers travelling on the ELR line between Bury and Summerseat.

It had been during the course of his second spell as PM that Peel in 1846, acting on conscience, played a central part in bringing about the repeal of the infamous *Corn Laws*. Since 1815, these laws had penalised the poorer classes of society who were forced to pay extra for bread on account of the tariff added to cheaper grain imports brought in from abroad.

Highly unpopular amongst his own Tory party colleagues for having taken an action which went against the vested interests of rich landowners, Peel had been constrained in the end to resign his post. At the same time, his brave intervention had been broadly applauded across the nation.

When news broke on 2 July 1850 that Peel had died following an accident whilst out riding his horse on Constitution Hill in London, widespread grief was felt and no more so than in the north-west of England. The Peel family's connection with Bury and neighbouring areas, such as the Burrs and Ramsbottom, struck a particular chord locally. A strong feeling emerged that some special form of tribute should be paid in honour of the illustrious former PM with roots so embedded in the Bury/Rossendale area.

Subsequently, a scheme had been devised to build an imposing tower astride Holcombe Hill. This was very much the brainchild of Grant Brothers, Daniel and John, who of course had previous experience to draw upon through involvement with construction of the family's special tribute to their own parents, namely Grants Tower. A committee of four prominent local businessmen was set up, including Tottington mill-owner Joshua Knowles, who had once worked for the Grants. With a backing sum of £1,000 raised from public subscription, the Peel Monument was built from millstone grit, quarried around its base. On completion, it was set to stand a towering 1,100 feet (335 metres) above sea level.

At the same time, another special commemorative monument had been projected for the centre of Bury. There, a statue of Peel, created by Sir Edward Hodges Baily (also known for his sculpture of Lord Nelson atop *Nelson's Column* in Trafalgar Square, London) had been unveiled the day before the official opening occasion of the Peel Monument on Holcombe Hill.

Attended by thousands of people, the ceremony on Holcombe Hill took place on 8 September 1852. Sir Robert Peel's son Frederick was the principal guest of honour. Notable speakers on the day included businessman and local JP John Robinson Kay as well as Joshua Knowles.

Although the occasion was attended in vast numbers, there were also unfortunately many who did not manage to arrive at the event on time, namely those who had travelled on 'excursion' trains. For example, the ELR had put on a special service scheduled to set off from Salford, stopping off en route at Radcliffe and Bury, before arriving at Ramsbottom Station. As however the *Bury Times* described in its report of happenings on the day: 'The event had commenced by the time the passengers had reached the station and the entire proceedings had terminated before they had ascended the hill.' [4]

Not enough time had been allowed for passengers to undertake the onward journey from the station to the site of the ceremony, which involved having to trek up a steep two-mile path through rough terrain to make it to the summit of Holcombe Hill. John Robinson Kay, in his capacity as an ELR company director, would not have been best pleased with the rail administrators responsible for this bungle. Peel Monument committee members Daniel and John Grant would also no doubt have had a 'pennyworth or two' to add of their own!

Pleasure Garden Excursions and the Rail Disaster of 1860

A highly popular type of rail excursion during these times was to pleasure gardens. The most famous was the one opened in 1836 by John Jennison at Belle Vue in Manchester where 36 acres of wasteland had been transformed into a veritable wonderland, including a zoo with star turns such as the '*King of Oudh's Fighting Tiger*' and a chimpanzee that smoked a pipe, drank tea and was dressed like a nobleman. There were many other attractions there besides, including a maze, a fine bowling green, pleasure boats upon a lake as well as extensive eating and drinking facilities.

Gradually over time, Jennison had also begun to put on events at special times, for example introducing a spectacular annual fireworks display – the first in 1852 – and also the September brass band contest which began in 1853.

Despite the enormous amount of pleasure over time that rail travellers derived from going on excursions to Belle Vue from Ramsbottom and a variety of other local places, one particular outing to Jennison's paradise was fated to end in tragedy. On 3 September, 1860, over 20,000 visitors from across the north of England attended the annual brass band competition put on that year. Several trains had been commissioned to pick up passengers from Ramsbottom and other adjacent locations such as Blackburn, Accrington, Burnley, Colne, Haslingden and Helmshore.

Passengers on those out-going trains no doubt enjoyed their day's experience at Belle Vue. In order to take them home in the late evening, three trains had been lined up, the first scheduled to set off at 22.45 pm, the second at 23.10 pm and the third at 23.31 pm. The first would carry 364 people to Ramsbottom before heading on towards Helmshore, then continuing on to Accrington and surrounding areas.

The second train was also heading for Ramsbottom before making its way to Helmshore. However, on arriving there at around 00.31 on Tuesday 4 September, it came to a sudden standstill. A rebound of the carriages caused a screw coupling and two side chains to snap, resulting in up to 17 loose carriages beginning to move backwards down the line in the direction which they had just travelled in.

The third train, having left Ramsbottom station, was on its way and passing the Ravenshore viaduct about 670 yards from Helmshore station. Meanwhile, the loose carriages from the second train had begun to gain momentum on the 1-in-100 incline. In the darkness of the night, as the third train passed over the viaduct, the carriages crashed into the oncoming engine of train number three.

At least ten of the loose carriages were smashed into smithereens in the collision with 11 people dead and over a hundred passengers suffering severe injuries. As well as all the internal rail inquiries that inevitably followed, tributes were paid to those who had lost their lives.

For example, an Ewood Bridge man who was killed, Samuel Duckworth, came to be buried in St. James Churchyard, Haslingden, his gravestone reading:

'In Memory of SAMUEL DUCKWORTH of Ewood Bridge who was killed in the HELMSHORE RAILWAY ACCIDENT Sept. 4th 1860 in his 50th year. Sudden and awful was the stroke. By which lives thread was broke. Oh haste to Christ make no delay. As no one knows their dying day.'

Notes
1. Chris Aspin, *Surprising Lancashire* pub. Helmshore Local History Society 1988, pp 40-1, based on a *Blackburn Standard* newspaper account of the incident at the time.
2. *Railway Times*, 1850, p. 659
3. *The Bacup Branch (Ramsbottom-Stubbins-Rawtenstall)* pub. L&YR Railway Society 1985, p.24
4. *Bury Times*, 10 September 1852

Map of Ramsbottom Station and its surrounding town area at the beginning of the 20th century.

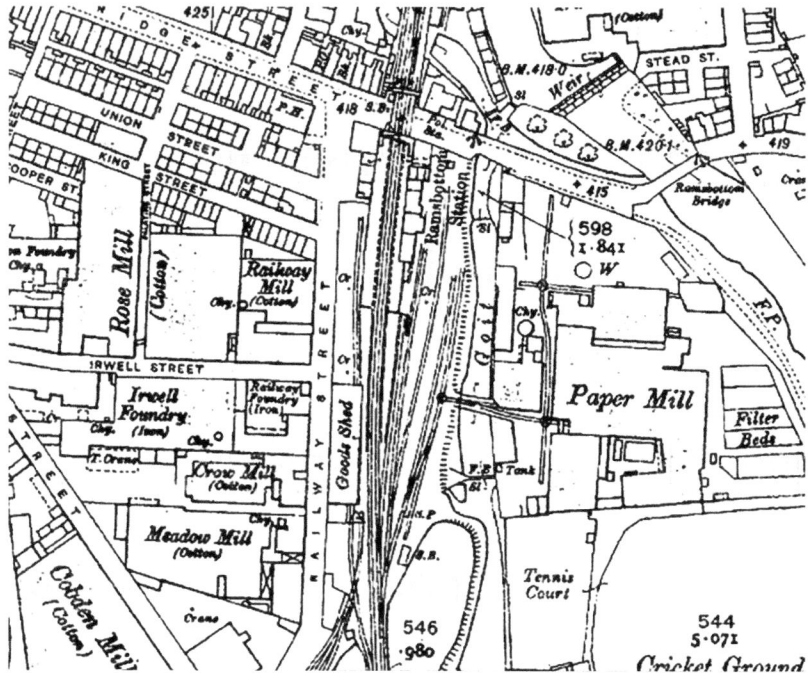

There are many interesting aspects to this map. Firstly, the number of sidings both to the west and east side of the station. The heavy industrial nature of the surrounding area can be seen through the number of cotton and paper mills and iron foundries. However, adverse economic circumstances in the second half of the 20th century onwards would cause the demise of these traditional industries, just as the railway station was eventually set to face closure itself. On a more social/sporting note, the tennis court area lasted until the end of the 1940s when it was dug up to make room for a new cricket Club House.

CHAPTER FIVE –

Part of the Lancashire & Yorkshire Railway up to 1923

Further growth of Ramsbottom as a railway town from the late 1850s onwards

In 1849, the ELR had provided eight trains each weekday from Salford to Bury together with two that started from Manchester Victoria. Six trains went on to Accrington. There were also six services to Newchurch, still at this time the terminus for the Rossendale line. Some of these involved a change of train at Ramsbottom. On Sundays there were five trains from Salford, three of which went through to Accrington and the other two to Newchurch. During the early years of L&YR ownership, all of the passenger train services had continued to run to Manchester via Clifton Junction.

Increased activity at Ramsbottom station came about when the L&YR decided to use the route through Ramsbottom as a viable alternative to its existing congested main line between Manchester and Leeds, adding considerably to the volume of traffic coming through the station. In addition, the L&YR began to filter much of its holiday traffic via Ramsbottom.

By the late 1850s, Ramsbottom had continued to grow quickly with many more factories opening. As well as increased demand from this direction, there was also a heightened interest in using the railway to bring in household goods, particularly food products. Prior to the age of refrigeration, as stated earlier, daily deliveries of perishable food arrived such as fish from Grimsby and Fleetwood.

The local haulage company of J & J Whittaker, founded by James Whittaker in 1825, had become so successful that by the end of the 1850s, the L&YR had granted them exclusive rights to carry goods from all the stations between Ramsbottom and Bacup. In return they were constrained to withdraw from the Manchester route.

Given all the different circumstances causing growth in station business, the L&YR saw fit to enhance facilities at Ramsbottom. By the early 1880s, there were 14 northbound weekday trains to Colne and the same number to Manchester Victoria. Work began during this decade on the establishment of a goods yard with sidings on both sides of the line running behind the two platforms.

In 1875, a signal box was installed on the north side of the level crossing, west of the line. This was supplemented by the later addition of a signal box on the Up side to the south of the station which controlled the sidings and goods yard. There were also two 'private' sidings. One of these served the bleaching works of Hepburn & Co., a firm which in the mid-60s had taken over the site of the Square Works after the Grants' business had closed down.

The background to this closure was that, after John and Daniel Grant both died in 1855, the business had been inherited by William and Robert Dalglish Grant, sons of John. Neither enjoyed good health though and Robert died in 1863. William, at a time when the effects of the American Civil War brought about a severe trade recession, had ended up selling the business. A similar fate befell the Ashtons' business enterprise at Ramsbottom Mill when the supply of raw cotton dried up during the *Lancashire Cotton Famine* of 1862-5. The second of the two 'private' sidings referred to above, which were accessed by a turntable from the goods yard, served the Ramsbottom Paper Mill on the east side.

Although the station's facilities were for the most part expanded upon during these years, the engine shed was closed down in 1882 when a new L&YR shed was opened at Bacup in that year. Further alterations to Rammy station included the construction in 1893 of a wooden footbridge, half-glazed and roofed, connecting up the two platforms at the level crossing end of the station. In terms of basic infrastructure, the station ended up being equipped with single-storey stone buildings on the Down platform, incorporating the main entrance, booking office, waiting rooms and staff facilities. A lengthy glazed canopy, of ridge and furrow design, extended from the north end of the platform for half the length of the station. On the southbound platform, single-storey brick and wooden buildings provided shelter for passengers and storage facilities for staff.

The Down side structures bore the hallmarks of what were classed as L&YR 'Style 2' in constructional terms. The booking hall was spacious with a skylight above. The Up side had the original buildings comprising the station master's house and the booking offices. The construction of more offices altered the original layout of the buildings.

Between the Down platform and Railway Street, there was a narrow yard, complete with two cranes of 10 ton and 30 hundredweight capacity. Behind the Up platform, there was a yard extending towards the paper mill, over which three dead-end sidings of different lengths passed. This yard had its opening near the main station buildings on Bridge Street guarded by a 12 ft. gate. Ramsbottom Paper Mill had two sidings in the yard separated from the other three sidings by a wall. There was a wagon turntable and siding running off at right-angles into the mill yard.

Meanwhile in 1860, the L&YR had built a new station at Summerseat. Constructed out of sandstone, it was single-storey with coupled round-headed windows (very much in Perring style) near each end of platform elevation. In 1875, a wooden signal box was opened at the north end of the northbound platform, replacing the box on the southbound platform.

In relation to Stubbins and Ewood Bridge stations, the original simple wooden buildings had been re-built in stone to include booking offices, waiting rooms and a station master's house. Ewood Bridge, which underwent a change of name to

Ewood Bridge & Edenfield in 1891, also had a siding with goods warehouse, weighing machine and crane.

Opening of the Bury to Holcombe Brook branch line in 1882
In the same way that Bury and Rossendale businessmen had in 1843 set up a company with the aim of creating a local rail connection, so in the 1870s manufacturers in the Tottington district, admittedly somewhat late in the day, looked to take active steps to protect their own district from being reduced to an industrial backwater.

Two of the prime movers behind this initiative were Richard Olive and Samuel Knowles. Born in 1837, Richard Olive was aged 43 by the time of the 1881 census and living with his wife and two children at the Springside property in Walmersley which had formerly been the residence of Grant brothers William and Daniel. He was the owner of a combined paper mill and wagon works.

Samuel Knowles was the younger step-brother of Joshua Knowles. In 1821, whilst still in his early 20s, Joshua had acquired Tottington cotton mill. He had extended the works so that by 1823, 300 people were employed there. By 1841, this had risen to 443, of whom 139 were children under the age of 13.

Joshua had constructed Tower Farm on the edge of Greenmount in 1840. This distinctive edifice was modelled on John Grant's Nuttall Hall Farm (Joshua had once worked at a Grant Brothers' mill in Ramsbottom and admired all they accomplished) with its fifty square feet castellated water tower and row of arches round the top, replicating the tops of medieval castle walls. The practical consideration behind building Tower Farm had been to stable the many heavy horses required during those times to bring coal from Affetside as well as transporting raw materials to, and finished goods from Tottington Mill, to Bury and elsewhere. It will be recalled that Joshua had played a leading role in the planning and organisation culminating in the opening of the Peel Monument on Holcombe Hill in 1852.

Following the death of Joshua in 1853, Samuel inherited his elder step-brother's various properties after the death of 'Joshua junior'. It was in the middle years of the 1870s that Samuel, in his mid-fifties and aware that the days of reliance on horse-and-cart transport were well and truly over, took it upon himself to form a railway company along with three other manufacturers in the area: Richard Olive of Woolfold, Edward Mucklow of Elton Fold and Hugh Roberts of Stormer Hill.

In 1876, the Bury and Tottington Railway Company had been formed with the aim of building a line stretching from Bury to Holcombe Brook. An Act of Parliament was passed on 2 August 1877 authorising the construction of the railway up as far as Holcombe Brook with added provision to incorporate a subsidiary line from Woolfold westwards to serve Richard Olive's wagon works.

It took until 6 November 1882 though before the line was opened for passenger and freight traffic. The main reason why it took four years stemmed from the many engineering exercises needing to be carried out, chiefly having to construct three viaducts. The first, comprising five skew arches built in stone, carried the line over the River Irwell shortly after leaving Tottington Junction. Another five-arch structure crossed the Kirklees Brook just before the station at Woolfold. Between Tottington and Greenmount, the largest viaduct crossed Scholes Lodge by means of nine arches. Out of Bury, the route climbed at a gradient of 1:50 most of the way, stepping up to 1:40 over the final mile.

Across the 3.75 mile length of track, there were various scheduled stops at Woodhill, Brandlesholme, Olive's, Woolfold, Sunnywood, Tottington, Knowles, Greenmount and Holcombe Brook. However, several of these stops were so-called 'halts' rather than stations, lacking proper platforms but relying on retractable steps being fitted to carriages to allow passengers to board and alight.

To celebrate the opening on 6 November 1882, Samuel Knowles and Hugh Roberts paid for all their employees to go on a day-trip to Belle Vue Gardens. Conventional services operated thereafter, consisting of a timetable of six midweek return trains running from Bury Bolton Street to Holcombe Brook, which were driven by L&YR steam engines. A working agreement between the BTDR and the L&YR granted the latter company

54% of the traffic receipts in return for BTDR's use of L&YR locomotive power and rolling stock.

Freight receipts were set to exceed those from the passenger side of the service by about a double amount. For example, passenger receipts in 1883 were £1,496 compared with freight at £2,855. In 1884, the figures were £1,352 and £2,822 respectively. Even though the BTDR branch line might have benefitted from the growing popularity of Holcombe Brook, given the added tourist attraction of the nearby Peel Monument, it still had to compete with the L&YR's rival stations at Ramsbottom and Summerseat, also quite conveniently situated in local terms. In addition, the branch line suffered from road competition, the steam tramway service between Bury and Tottington beginning in 1883.

The BTDR's independence was to come to an end by an act of Parliament passed on 24 July 1888 after just less than six years of operation. From this time on, the L&YR took over full control of the branch line.

Competition further increased with the introduction in 1904 of electric trams run by Bury Corporation. 'In response to this, the L&YR decided to introduce steam railmotors on the branch in an attempt to win back passengers.'[1]

Steam railmotors, designed and built by Kerr, Stuart & Co., began running on the Holcombe Brook branch line on 3 July 1905. A further chapter of development opened when the line was electrified in 1913. The context of how this happened was that the Preston-based firm now known as Dick, Kerr & Co., in process of considering putting in a tender for an electrification contract in Brazil, was looking for somewhere more local to test matters out. The result was that this relatively obscure branch line ended up enjoying the distinction of being one of the first high-voltage electric railways in the world.

Introduction of Electric Trolley Bus Service and *Little Billie*

Ramsbottom Urban District Council introduced an electric trolley bus service which opened on 14 August 1913. It ran from *The Hare and Hounds* in Holcombe Brook to Market Place, Ramsbottom and then on to Edenfield.

James Spencer was later to recall: 'These were single-decker buses ('trackless trams') with solid tyres, not very well sprung, and driven on cobbled roads, resulting in a very rough ride for the passengers. They were powered by electricity from overhead cables slung from iron pillars at intervals on each side of the road. In the winter when the roads were icy a bus would skid off the road and into someone's front garden.' [2]

Another bus service ran from Market Pace to Ramsbottom station. However, this added leg was to prove short-lived, being abandoned on 5 October 1914 soon after the outbreak of the 1914-18 war. The service from Holcombe Brook to Edenfield was to go on running until it was closed down on 31 March 1931.

In 1914, the L&YR introduced a 'Rail-motor' service – known locally as *'Little Billie'* – between Ramsbottom and Bacup. This called at all stations and supplemented trains that ran through to Manchester. From 11 April 1916, through passenger services to Manchester from the Bacup branch were diverted once more, this time to travel via Heywood, adding considerable mileage to their journey. The reason for this was that from this date, electric services began on the Bury to Manchester (via Prestwich) line. Passengers for Manchester travelling on these services were encouraged to change on to electric trains at Bury for a quicker onward journey, and most of them did.

Outbreak of World War One: 1914
The conflagration that had started in 1914 was set to last through until 1918. Inevitably, it meant that local matters paled into insignificance in comparison to the scale of challenge now facing the nation by way of committing to a war abroad. With railways coming under state control, the system was vital to the war effort in terms of transporting troops, horses, military equipment and medical supplies to ports around the country.

As far as the threat to Britain's home population was concerned, the effect was relatively minor, certainly by comparison with what was to transpire during the course of World War II. However, for people living in Rossendale, the night of 25 September 1916 was to be remembered for a civilian air offensive when L21, a huge Zeppelin airship which had entered the country over the

Lincolnshire coast, threatened Rossendale before moving on to Bolton. The first damage of any real significance occurred with regard to rail lines when a salvo of five explosive and two incendiary bombs were dropped at Ewood Bridge with a section of track destroyed just north of Irwell Vale Bridge.

Then, after passing over Helmshore, the Zeppelin, commanded by Oberleutnant Kurt Frankenberg of the Imperial German Navy, dropped five more bombs on Holcombe on its way to Bolton. Holcombe Post Office suffered considerable damage. The *Shoulder of Mutton* public house had twenty of its windows shattered and its front door broken in half. A further bomb fell by the gable (Helmshore end) of Holcombe School, causing severe damage, also breaking the church clock and smashing windows. The sole casualty of this part of the raid was in fact a thrush, the body of which was preserved by a taxidermist and thereafter kept on exhibit in a glass case.

It was thought that the Zeppelin pilot's original target had been industrial Manchester but that, confused about directions, bombs were randomly discharged over any communication lines that came into view such as the railway track at Ewood Bridge. Fortunately, Rossendale suffered no human casualties in what the *Rossendale Free Press* would play down as 'a night-time bombing raid that went wrong'. [3]

However, the civilian death toll from the Zeppelin attack that night was to reach thirteen in Bolton, 'made up of five men, five women and three young girls aged seventeen, five and two.' [4]

By way of postscript, just over two months later, in the early morning of 28 November 1916, 29-year-old Frankenberg and his L21 were shot down in flames off Lowestoft by a British aeroplane after carrying out a bombing raid in West Yorkshire and the Staffordshire Pottery Towns.

For the major part of the war, the challenge of keeping the domestic rail system going critically depended upon women taking over. Huge gaps occurred in the workforce in the light of 100,000 male workers being enlisted as soldiers and going abroad to fight. By the end of the war, there were over 65,000 women employed on the railways with over half employed in "male roles".

As far as the L&YR was concerned, the company 'had employed only just over 1,000 women prior to 1914 but by November 1918 had increased the number of women employed in "ladies'" roles by another 64, whilst also employing over 3,300 women in "male grades". [5]

'An Incident without precedent at Ramsbottom'
As reported in the *'Bacup Times'* on 17 January 1920, the following 'incident' occurred at Ramsbottom:

'The coaches forming the 6.05 train were placed in a siding and, during the night, a mouse got into the vacuum valve of the Guard's van. On the engine being attached to the coaches, it was found impossible to get the vacuum brake to act. The mouse was found but could not be extricated and, after a delay of nine minutes, it is stated that the train went to Bacup without brake control over the last three carriages. About a day was required to put the vacuum apparatus in order again and a lengthy report was required by the railway authorities.' [6]

Notes
1. *The Holcombe Brook Branch*, 1988 – No. 6 in the Branch lines of the L&YR series – pub. L&YR Society p.18
2. James Spencer, *Ramsbottom in the early 1900s*, an article in Ramsbottom Reminiscences Vols. 1&2, pub. 2022 by Ramsbottom Heritage Society (ed. Andrew Todd) p.8
3. *Rossendale Free Press*, 27 September 1916
4. Peter JC Smith, 1991, *Zeppelins Over Lancashire*, pub. Neil Richardson, p.20
5. Linda Henderson, *'Not a job for a woman?'* an article in January 2015 ELR News Magazine p. 90
6. Peter Lord article in Summer/Autumn 1991 ELR News Magazine – *'Trouble on't Line'* - based on a *Bacup Times* report of 17 January 1920.

John Shae Perring 1813-69 Egyptologist and Rail Engineer

Last day of the Peel Bridge Tollgate - Friday 26 October 1900

View of Bridge Street from Level Crossing - photo taken post WW2

J and J Whittaker ply their trade

Inside Ramsbottom Station April 1954

Cottrill's convey goods to the station

Outside view of Ramsbottom's original station of 1846 - photo taken in 1960s

Ramsbottom Station from the level crossing in the 1960s

Dr Beeching presents his crushing report 1963

Police presence at Summerseat Station - Jan 1967

Ramsbottom Station one week before closure in 1972

June 1972, the last passenger train from Ramsbottom Station

State of Ramsbottom Station in June 1984

Breaking through the banner at Bury Bolton Street on 25 July 1987

Crowds cheer arrival of train at Ramsbottom Station on 25 July 1987

Station Master Dave Greenwood (Rammy) greets Harry Hatcher (Bury counterpart)
25 07 1987

Gothenburg ELR No.1 at Ramsbottom Station 25 07 1987

The Clan Grant Pipe Band from Grantown - on- Spey performing 25 07 1987

CHAPTER SIX –

Wakes Weeks excursions and arrival of evacuees at start of World War II

New Government strategy brings in the *'Big Four'*
Following the end of World War I, the Government took a decision to rationalise the running of railways. At the time of the outbreak of war, there had been as many as 120 separate railway companies operating across Britain. To avoid service duplication and try to make rail provision more efficient, the ruling coalition government under Prime Minister David Lloyd George, in the aftermath of the end of war, carried out a *Railway Act* amalgamating all those 120 companies into four larger regional companies. The so-called *'Big Four'* consisted of: the Great Western Railway (GWR), the London, Midland & Scottish (LMS), the London & North Eastern Railway (LNER) and the Southern Railway (SR). On 1 January 1923, Ramsbottom thus came under the authority of the LMS as opposed to the now defunct L&YR.

'Goods Train Smash' in August 1923
However, it was a railway accident taking place in Ramsbottom in the early hours of 17 August 1923, fortunately without loss of life that became the first main occurrence to capture newspaper headlines during the initial year that East Lancashire rail lines came under LMS authority. The event was described as follows in a report published the day after:

'Shortly before two o'clock, a goods train weighing some 600 tons left Earby for Salford, travelling via Accrington. When going down the gradient beyond Haslingden station the driver was unable to apply the brakes…with the result that the train got out of control and dashed along the track at a speed of little less than sixty miles an hour, finally coming to grief in the Ramsbottom station goods yard, into which it had been turned from the main line owing to the presence of mind of a points man.

'In the goods yard the train dashed into a number of goods wagons, which were practically demolished, and then crashed into the district engineer's office and the store rooms. The force of the collision was such that the fore part of the goods train was telescoped by the crash and the district engineer's offices standing alongside the line were wrecked. Both passenger lines were blocked by the wreckage for some time.

'The driver and fireman had miraculous escapes and jumped from the engine to save their lives. They are W. Aughton (35) of 10, Broadhurst Road, Newton Heath, Manchester, the driver, who suffered concussion and abrasions on the head, and fireman Herbert Bannister (23) of Knowle Square, Hollinwood, who received deep gashes on the cheek and chin, and abrasions on the arms.

'Luckily, the local police station was close to the scene of the mishap, and the police were thus quickly at hand to render aid to the two injured men. Dr Crompton was summoned and ordered the men to be removed to Ramsbottom Cottage Hospital.

'The stationmaster, Mr Richard Kay, quickly got in hand the necessary work for clearing the permanent way, with the result that there was little or no delay to passenger traffic. Police officers who heard the train running at an excessive speed said the crash sounded like a row of houses toppling over. PS Wren and PC Walker heard an engine whistle sounding in a peculiar manner from the direction of Helmshore.

'Thinking something must be wrong, they immediately hurried towards the station. When they got about a hundred yards from the Market Place they heard a long crash. On arriving at the railway they found the engine almost buried under a pile of trucks. PC Walker went along the railway line, and found the fireman lying in a dazed condition.

'Higher up the line, he came across the driver, who was practically unconscious. Both men were carried into the Police Station. The debris on the side of the railway was piled over 20 feet high.'[1]

Despite the line's changing hands into LMS authority, the same tendency had shown up yet again for incidence of steep gradients to lead to 'runaway trains' careering out of control.

Ramsbottom station timetable during the Inter-War years
Taking 1932 as an example, the station had 39 northbound services on weekdays; thirteen of them went to Colne, three to Accrington, one to Rose Grove, one went to Stubbins and the rest went to Bacup. There was also a service that arrived from Bury and terminated at 5.50 am at Ramsbottom. The first northbound service was for Stubbins, and it left Ramsbottom at 5.42 am. The last service which had originated from Bury Bolton Street left Rammy for Bacup at 11.27 pm.

Meanwhile, 38 trains travelled south from Ramsbottom on weekdays, five to Bury Bolton Street and four terminated at Bury Knowsley Street. Twenty-nine trains went to Manchester Victoria. Ten of these went via Heywood while nineteen took the more direct route via Clifton Junction. The first southbound departure was for Bury Bolton Street at 5.44 am. The last was also for Bury Bolton, leaving at 10.37 pm.

Excursions and *Wakes Weeks*
In addition to the trains listed in the public timetable, there were the excursion and holiday trains. When holidays with pay became the norm after the First World War, the practice was for each local Lancashire town to hold a '*Wakes Week*' when most employers would shut down their works for the week.

As Margaret Ferguson was later to recall: 'I should think that at least 90% of the local population went on holiday in the annual Wakes Week, mostly to Blackpool, or St Anne's if you were slightly more posh, whilst the really posh went to Colwyn Bay,

Rhyl or Llandudno…The whole of Ramsbottom seemed to shut down, every mill, every shop, no papers, no bread, no nothing!

'My Dad being a railway employee was allowed a certain number of free passes every year…Sometimes Mam would take me to Blackpool for the day, and if it were Wakes Week, arrangements were made to see Auntie Alice and Uncle Jack, and have our dinner at their digs.' [2]

Ramsbottom and the Lancashire Cricket League
Another means by which railway services received a fair boost in East Lancashire during these years stemmed from the period marking a heyday in the popularity of Lancashire League cricket. The championship at this time came to be dominated by Nelson, clinching the winners' trophy at will from 1928 onwards and virtually throughout the 30s. Their star player was West Indian all-rounder Learie Constantine. His arrival in 1929 'sparked a run of highly dramatic batting and bowling feats…and also attracted ever-increasing numbers to pay their money at the gate to watch him perform.' [3]

Special trains were put on to accommodate the huge crowds travelling to see matches involving Nelson/Constantine, conveying thousands of passengers. It put a lot of pressure on the local rail stations of host cricket clubs. At Ramsbottom for example, special arrangements were made with trains being stabled in the loops to the north of the level crossing.

Life in the signal box
Fred Hanson, a signalman at Rammy during these illustrious cricketing times, later recalled fondly: 'the local signalmen had their own grandstand view of the match. Ramsbottom South Box stood by the old Square Works, overlooking Acre Bottom cricket ground, and the men had put in their own 18-inch square window in the back of the box. On match day Sundays, when the box might be manned for an engineer's possession, the rostered signalman would have nothing to do but watch the game.

'Meanwhile on Saturday afternoons, *Cottrill's* stand would sell hundreds of pork pies' (baked in a shop at the top end of Dungeon Row on Bridge Street, now the site of *Woodholme*

Supplies at nos. 40-42). 'There were times', added Fred, 'when you couldn't get into the cricket ground and you'd have to go over to the *Cheeky Stand* (a patch of land nearby lying on the opposite bank of the River Irwell) where, without having to pay an entry fee, you could still see what was happening on the field of play even if from something of a greater distance away'. On one occasion, Constantine 'scattered some of the illicit spectators in the Cheeky Stand by hitting a ball for six over the river and amongst them.' [4]

Fred, having worked in both of the Ramsbottom crossing boxes, remembered the old L&YR model as 'poky, a queer little hole…The steps up to the old box were near to the pavement and in the ginnel by the footbridge. They were moved in the 1938/9 reconstruction to stop drunks coming up and mithering the signalman.' He further recalled: 'Oil lamps inside before the 1930s, then gaslights, heavy levers facing the line, very limited clearance around the wheel which was parallel with the tracks, so you had to move front and back of it to get a view up and down the street.'

There were domestic comforts though: 'A pot-bellied stove heated the box, best Yorkshire coal was the favourite, and soon got white hot, and on the top was the kettle, perpetual hot water! Engine drivers dropped off the odd cod or two. Also every signalman had a tin for cooking bacon, steak in a minimum of time. My favourite being a large onion cut small and fried until brown with butter then drop the cheese in, slap it on two rounds of real bread (homemade). Brill! That in one hand and pull levers, ring bells, answer phone and swing wheel as necessary with other.' [5]

In harsher terms, Fred remembered Ramsbottom's gates as being exposed to the wind, and in consequence often being 'heavy' to swing, at the same time recalling trainee signalmen who were frightened of not being able to get the gates open to the railway in time for approaching trains because of the number of people crossing. The discovery early one May morning in 1932 of the dead body of signalman Joseph Richards in the box's chair, who was later diagnosed to have died from cardiac failure, served to heighten the tensions associated with carrying out the job. [6]

Railway Goods Traffic

It is difficult in the present day to imagine the sheer scale and range of goods traffic activity carried out around the station and its extensive sidings network at this earlier point in time. For example, a whole series of stone and coal yards stretched to the north of the station along Stubbins Lane adjacent to the six coal sidings, which lay on the western side of the railway line. [7]

Going back as far as 1846, the advent of rail had facilitated the exporting of stone from the dozens of quarries in the area to a then ever-growing market of northern cities. Methods of conveyance of such raw materials had remained fairly rudimentary over intervening time. Relating to coal, it was later recalled how in 1935 this raw material 'was still hauled from the railway yards to the mills by two-wheeled carts drawn by huge Belgian draft horses and Clydesdales. I would go round to the smithy on Paradise Street and watch them being shod. They were so big that as a child I could walk under their bellies.' [8]

The much larger extent of sidings on the east side had been laid out around the 1880s to the east of the Stubbins line. The land chosen for the sidings, Great Eaves Meadow, to the north of Ramsbottom station, was the only flat site in the area with sufficient acreage and accessibility. Known as Ramsbottom Marshalling Sidings, they were used for making up goods trains rather than transhipment from other forms of feeder transport.' [9]

World War Two: arrival of evacuees by rail

In the face of the prospect of war breaking out again in 1939, one of the first basic needs was to evacuate children away from city areas where they were at great risk from bombing raids. The railway system played a crucial part in the safeguarding process.

For example, many young children left the Newton Heath district of Manchester to be billeted in the Ramsbottom area. Margaret Hammersley later recalled the children arriving a few days after war had been declared on 3 September of that year: 'When the evacuees came from Newton Heath, I was in the St. John's Ambulance and was at the station to meet the train. Many townspeople stood in the street weeping openly at the sight of the children with their gas masks. They were taken to St. Paul's and eventually found accommodation'. [10]

An evacuee arriving a bit earlier than this, Eric Quinn described his experience as follows: 'It was Friday 1 September 1939 about 8.30 am. I was 8 years and 11 months…We were walked across to Victoria Station and put on a steam train. We did not know where we were going. We all carried a gas mask and a haversack. I was not frightened as I had my big brother with me. We arrived in Ramsbottom. I thought the train station was marvellous compared to Newton Heath. It had a big canopy and a big booking office. We waited lined up outside The Railway Hotel.' [11]

Another evacuee, Geoff Hall, who was billeted in Summerseat, remembered 'listening to the wireless, on Sunday morning 3 September 1939, as Prime Minister Neville Chamberlain announced that we were at war with Germany'. Recollecting his general experience, he said later that 'I have good and vivid memories of those days, including riding on *Puffing Billy* from Summerseat, through the tunnel to Ramsbottom, on a Saturday afternoon to go to the pictures.' [12]

Incidentally, the cinema Geoff would have attended was most likely the *Empire Picture Palace* on Railway Street (which closed in the 1960s and is now the site of '*Clark's Craft*' store). Although not an evacuee herself, Doris Hibbert recalled later 'what a treat it was going to the cinema – taking us to the magical world of exciting stories, romance, music and dancing. Fourpence ha'penny (4½ d) was the price of a child's ticket. Of course we had to go in the black-out. Gosh, the streets were dark.' [13]

Goods of every sort possible still invariably came by rail. Unlikely-sounding but highly illustrative of the times, Marlene Crowley was later to recall how as a child she had been thrilled by a particular box being delivered via the railway to her granddad: 'Inside the box were new-born fluffy yellow chicks and these were put on the peg rug (which Grandma had made out of pieces of old coats) to keep them warm in front of the fire. Granddad let each of us children choose one and give it a name, but because they all looked the same, we soon forgot which our special one was. This proved to be a blessing really as this was the time of rationing and eventually they all ended up as Sunday dinner.' [14]

With the railway system having a major role to play in the transfer of troops and armaments, ordinary passenger traffic was discouraged, backed by slogans such as '*Is Your Journey Really Necessary?*' Whilst fares remained the same for people travelling to a workplace, increases were imposed on fares for those engaged in a leisure outing. With the state taking full control again in the same way it had done during World War I, it was relatively straightforward to implement. For example, basic return fares from Ramsbottom to Bury were increased from 7½d to 9 ½d.' [15]

Meanwhile, the town was protected from potential threat of invasion by its Home Guard – or else known officially – the '*Local Defence Volunteers*'. Unofficially this more posh title was under-scored as: '*Look, Duck and Vanish*'. [16]

Railway nationalisation in 1948

The longer the war lasted, the stronger the feeling grew on the Government's part that there should be no post-war return of rail control into the hands of private companies. The inter-war '*Big Four*' arrangement had not proved a success even if it had to be conceded the system had suffered from massive under-investment.

At the end of World War II, the Labour Party had won the 1945 election with a landslide majority and taken the opportunity to seek to nationalise Britain's run-down railway system. With the plan finally being given the green light by Parliament, the 1947 *Transport Act* created the *British Transport Commission* to oversee the modernisation and integration not only of rail but also road, canal and air transport. From 1 January 1948, the railways were run by a body called the *Railway Executive*, answerable to the *BTC*.

However, the newly-created British Railways (BR) not only found itself faced with the enormous task of needing to repair about 20,000 miles of worn-out track and related infrastructure, but also of modernising its stock of over 20,000 steam engines, over one million goods wagons and over 55,000 passenger carriages.

BR's *Modernisation Plan* of 1955

Apart from anything else, 'modernisation' spelt the end of steam locomotives and replacement by diesel-electric locomotives. The new programme targeted in particular the development of lightweight diesel trains – *DMUs* (diesel multiple units).

Ramsbottom found itself very much projected into the spotlight after the Bury to Bacup line was selected as one of the first in the country to receive the new DMUs. The first trial was carried out in 1954 using a *Derby lightweight* with further testing taking place during 1955. The plan was for these units to replace the steam-hauled Bacup/Bury/Manchester service via Heywood and Moston and also the Bury to Bacup services from 6 February 1956 onwards.

Bury Shed took delivery of seven twin car sets built by Metro Cammell. Numbered *79076 – 82 (motor coach) and 79626 – 32 (driving trailer)*, precursors of the large 101 fleet which followed. It was in August 1955 that the first lightweight diesel car, produced by Metro Cammell, had emerged from Washwood Heath works at Saltley in Birmingham.

The sets allocated to Bury worked regular trips to Manchester Victoria during December 1955 and January 1956. A formal demonstration run was made on 31 January 1956 from Manchester to Bacup. From Bury to Bacup, the weekday services doubled to half-hourly frequency with 35 trains on weekdays and 47 on Saturdays with the journey time reduced from 37 to 34 minutes.

From the first six days of operation, 23,000 passengers travelled, compared with 8,000 in the same period by steam in the previous year. Later figures released in July 1956 showed 156,317 passengers had travelled on the Bury-Bacup line since the diesel service had started on 6 February 1956, an increase in take-up of 35%, seeming to demonstrate the potential of the diesel service to revive the fortunes of local rail routes.

'Fierce blaze' at Ramsbottom station on Christmas Day morning 1958

'But for the prompt action of a passer-by in summoning the Fire Brigade, Ramsbottom Railway Station booking office, with bags of late Christmas mail awaiting dispatch, might have been destroyed in a fierce blaze early on Christmas morning.

'Ramsbottom and Rawtenstall Fire Brigades raced to the station to find that flames had got a good hold. It took them about 20 minutes to put out the blaze. Cupboards and a book rack were burnt out, windows broken and the whole of the ceiling was damaged, but the mail bags, at the other end of the office from which the fire apparently started, were untouched. A large stock of tickets was destroyed.

'It was about three a.m. when the passer-by Mr. Joseph Nolan, of 61 Poplar Grove, Ramsbottom, noticed a glare in the booking office window. Using the telephone kiosk just outside the station, he put emergency calls through to Ramsbottom Fire Brigade and Ramsbottom Police Station. Ramsbottom Fire Brigade arrived six minutes after receiving the call.

'Said Ramsbottom Stationmaster, Mr. Ronald Hirst: "If the passer-by had not seen the glare through the window, the office would have been destroyed. The station was closed and no staff were on duty." [17]

The circumstances of "windows broken" naturally raised suspicions as to whether it was a break-in that had gone wrong. The fact that certain folk might well have been out and about in town the worse for wear after a long bout of Christmas Eve celebrating adds fuel to such thoughts, particularly if the mail bags had been open to view from outside.

With no record though of further information available regarding the occurrence, the evidence on the face of it did appear to confirm that Joseph Nolan's alertness in calling in the emergency services played a pivotal part in saving the station from being completely destroyed by the 'fierce blaze'.

The Swan Song of *Wakes Weeks*, Excursion Trains and Nuttall Village

Railway services in the early 1960s had continued operating longer distance steam-hauled trains services, including the *Wakes Weeks* holiday trains to Blackpool, Morecambe and St. Anne's. Fortnight-long *Wakes Weeks* for the Ramsbottom area were the first two weeks in July, although previously having taken place during August.

Rail travellers such as Alan Heywood retained evocative memories long after of weekend evening trips at this time to Blackpool which left Ramsbottom around 4.30 pm and arrived back there at 2 am. 'Certain travellers would unscrew the light bulbs and chuck them out of the train on the return journey – giving rise to the train's nickname: the "passion wagon". [18]

Meanwhile, other recollections of this particular period in time further reveal curious goings-on from rail-side life. For example, residents of Nuttall seemed in the habit of going down to the railway line below Starling Street to collect coal that 'dropped off' the trains. This enabled them to burn the coal on the fires that heated their houses.

One theory for the dropping-off of the coal was that train drivers knew local station-cleaner Marion Blundell lived close by. It was believed to be for her benefit that they chucked pieces of coal out of the cab. Marion herself appears to have been something of an intrepid soul, 'used to walking to work from her house along the railway line through the tunnel pushing herself back into the wall if a train came by. Her journey was not approved of and, after she witnessed a swan being killed on the railway line, she stopped using that route.' [19]

The more conventional route provided for pedestrians was the one often referred to during these times as *going over the Nuts*, the cobbled path built to ensure continued foot access between Summerseat and Nuttall, undertaken on the back of the building of the Brooksbottom and Nuttall Tunnels back in the mid-1840s.

Just as *Wakes Weeks* and excursion trains were set to enter into decline in the 1960s, so the existence of old-established communities came under threat. Take the village of Nuttall for example. Once it had been a thriving settlement with approximately 124 households (cottages) and 880 residents recorded in the census of 1841. The village's demise had begun to set in from the early 20th century onwards. By the start of the 1960s it was almost complete.

The last remaining residences in Nuttall village's Starling Street, known locally as *Shepsters*, or *Shebby Row* - '*shepster*' being the dialect for starling – were eventually demolished in 1962. Meanwhile, the Nuttall Hall farm buildings were destined to remain intact until the mid-1970s when they too were demolished to make way for the Broad Hey/Whittingham Drive housing estate constructed by building company Wimpey.

Notes

1. *Accrington Observer*, 18 August 1923
2. Margaret Ferguson, *A Rammy Childhood 1924-34*, an article in *Ramsbottom Reminiscences Vols 1&2*, pub. Ramsbottom Heritage Society (ed. Andrew Todd) pp. 116-7
3. Nigel Jepson, *175 Not Out – The Story of Ramsbottom Cricket Club*, pub. 2022 by YouCaxton p.34
4. Andrew Todd article in Winter 2019 ELR News Magazine: *Memories of Ramsbottom Signalbox and Crossings*, p.22
5. As for Item 4, also p.22
6. *Ramsbottom Observer*, 20 May 1932
7. Andrew Todd, *Railway Goods Traffic at Ramsbottom*, an article in RHS News Magazine No. 64 Spring/Summer 2023 p. 15
8. Alan Slater, *Ramsbottom Ramblings*, an article in RHS News Magazine No. 24 Spring 2003 p. 13
9. As for Item 6 above
10. *Ramsbottom Heritage Society Commemorative War News*, pub. 2010 – Issue 1: *Preparing for War* p.5
11. *RHS War News* – Issue 1: *Preparing for War* p.7
12. *RHS War News* – Issue 1: *Preparing for War* p.5
13. *RHS War News* – Issue 5: *1943* p. 9
14. Marlene Crowley, *Memories of Pebble Beach*, an article in RHS News Magazine No. 25 Autumn 2003 pp. 15/16
15. *RHS War News* – Issue 4: 1942 p. 15
16. Herbert H Duckworth, *Memories of Jobs in Ramsbottom, 1925-65*, an article in *Ramsbottom Reminiscences Vols 1&2*, pub. Ramsbottom Heritage Society (ed. Andrew Todd) p. 81
17. *Bury Times*, 3 January 1959
18. *Nuttall – Ramsbottom's Lost Village*, 2020, pub. Ramsbottom Heritage Society, p. 57
19. As for Item 18 above, also p. 57

CHAPTER SEVEN -

Taking a hit from the *'Beeching Cuts'* of the 1960s

Hatchet Job on Railways
Since the demise of the original ELR in 1859, there had been various changes along the way in terms of how the railway set-up at Ramsbottom was managed. First, it had come under the authority of the L&YR then, after 1923, the LMS. More recently, since nationalisation, it was British Railways. However, during the 1960s, the railway network as a whole was to be subjected to a further bout of change – one destined to be far wider-ranging and more threatening. As far as Ramsbottom was concerned, its identity as a railway town suddenly looked in serious jeopardy.

The starting-point to these wide-ranging changes came in the form of the Government's *Transport Act* of 1962. The Act set up a *British Railways Board* with the aim of dealing with deficits incurred in running the national railway system. The appointment of Dr Richard Beeching to chair the Board was a controversial one due to the fact he had never previously worked in the railway industry. It was all part of the Government's thinking though to bring someone in to tackle the problem whose approach would be 'outside the box'.

Beeching's substantive post was as a scientist with *ICI*. He took on the role of Chairman of the *British Railways Board* on a secondment basis. He was to return to *ICI* after carrying out the 'hatchet job' on the railway system that the Government expected of him. In the *Report* he produced in 1963, *'The Re-shaping of*

British Railways', Beeching did not fall short of Government expectations by identifying 2,263 stations and 5,000 miles of track nationwide for closure. This amounted to 55% of existing stations, 30% of route mileage, with 67,700 jobs to be shed.[1]

Earlier rail closures in East Lancashire
Not that the *'Beeching Cuts'* of the 1960s were exactly a new phenomenon in terms of rail closures. For example, in East Lancashire, Haslingden station had already been closed to passengers in 1960. Its isolated location on the edge of town had always been a disadvantage as far as passenger traffic was concerned. The declared reason for closure was the unnecessary cost of station staff. The station was closed for freight goods in 1964.

The Bury to Holcombe Brook branch was another example of cutbacks pre-Beeching. In 1938, there had been 29 return trips on weekdays but the advent of motor buses in 1948, in place of Bury's tramway service, 'hammered the last nail into the branch line's coffin.'[2]

From carrying 52,000 passengers in 1946, this amount had plummeted to 25,000 by 1950. In fact, it reached the point when there was only one day a year that the operation could really be said to be busy. This was on Good Friday when it was local tradition for folk from the Bury area to make the trek up Holcombe Hill.

The branch service had continued on into BR days but on 25 March 1951 its electric trains were replaced by steam push-pulls, pending anticipated renewal of the electrical equipment. However, the overhaul never took place and the passenger service had been completely withdrawn on 4 May 1952. Goods traffic continued to be handled until 1960 when the branch was cut back from Bury to Tottington.

This truncated stretch of the branch line survived only until August 1963, never thereafter to be restored to use as a railway. By way of postscript, the extinct railway line linking Greenmount and Bury town centre was destined to become known in later times as the *'Kirklees Trail'*, providing pathway access through the

Kirklees Valley Local Nature Reserve for the benefit of walkers and cyclists.

Effects of Beeching Plan on East Lancashire
As in the case of so many other towns and stations up and down the country, the *'Beeching Cuts'* were ultimately to seal Ramsbottom's own fate in terms of rail connection. As far as the Bury area in general was affected, the Report could hardly have been more threatening. Closure notices were published concerning huge slices of routes from Clifton Junction through Bury to Bacup and Accrington.

Meanwhile, a 'saving' clause had been built in to the Report, allowing rail travellers the right to respond to its findings. Bodies were set up to handle public reaction, called *Transport Users' Consultative Committees (TUCCs)*. Not surprisingly, the closure notices aroused a lot of opposition.

Local reactions to Beeching findings
Amidst widespread dissent, the residents of Summerseat were most notably up in arms, mainly relating to the lines from Bury to Bacup and Accrington. The argument was strongly put forward that their village now lay in serious danger of being cut off and that any proposed alternative bus service failed to take account of the fact that road access to and from Summerseat was very difficult due to steep gradients.

There seemed precious little urgency though on the part of the Government reacting to rail travellers' responses to closure notices. When final decisions were eventually announced in September 1966, there were mixed feelings in Ramsbottom on outcomes. On the negative side, it was confirmed the line from Stubbins Junction to Accrington was set to close. Rather more positively, the stretch from Bury Bolton Street to Rawtenstall (the rump of the original ELR line of 1846) appeared to have been reprieved…

Events in Helmshore: 1966
When closure of the Ramsbottom/Accrington line was announced, the decision was reacted to adversely. In particular,

it incurred the displeasure of a significant group of people in Helmshore who would now no longer be able to commute by rail to Manchester.

Letters fired off by way of protest to the Prime Minister and to the Secretary of State for Transport produced a disappointing response to the effect that there could be no interference with the decision already announced. As something of a last throw of the dice, a public meeting had been arranged to take place in Helmshore on 25 November 1966, shortly before the scheduled closure of the line.

Although at the time, people in Ramsbottom might have been forgiven for thinking all of what was happening here had little to do with them, events were destined to show the opposite.

To continue the on-going story! With the intention in mind to form a Helmshore and District Railway Preservation Society (H&DRPS), Walter Baker was chosen to address the meeting. Baker had strong experience of dealing with similar situations, being a prominent member of West Yorkshire's Keighley and Worth Valley Railway Preservation Society (KWVRPS). The Society had been formed after the closure of the Keighley and Worth Valley Railway in 1962. KWVRPS had been successful in buying back the line from BR, who had allowed the Society to pay the sum in instalments. It was now on the point of re-opening it as a heritage railway, a goal that was set to come to fruition on 29 June 1968.

Having so much relevant experience behind him, Baker was persuasive in putting his case forward at the Helmshore meeting. By the end of it, an eight-member Helmshore Society Council had been formed, including three representatives of the local authority, Haslingden Corporation. The purpose was declared to be to secure the continued existence of the passenger commuter section of line from Stubbins to Accrington.

However, on Saturday 3 December 1966, the last trains had made their final runs on three local condemned lines, including that from Stubbins to Accrington. At Helmshore, the sole surviving station on the line, hundreds of local people and enthusiasts turned out on the day to mark the occasion. The train bore the same coat of arms as the original East Lancashire

Railway Company did on the occasion that the line had been opened back in 1848.

Whilst Walter Baker and his team of supporters continued to fight the cause, BR slammed the door in their face by imposing harsh terms on any proposed way forward. With support from local councillors waning, it was not long before the H&DRPS came to resurrect itself as the East Lancashire Railway Preservation Society, starting looking for possible alternative ways forward beyond Helmshore.

Summerseat Protest Event: 1967
Meanwhile, when it was originally announced that the Bury-Bacup line would be closed under the Beeching cuts, there had been similar strong protests from the villagers of Summerseat. A *Rail Action Committee* was formed with the aim of publicising their concerns. This entailed contacting everyone who could be thought of to help in the matter, even leading to a letter being dispatched to the United Nations.

The villagers, who had enjoyed support from neighbouring towns including Ramsbottom, were understandably jubilant when the announcement was made in September 1966 by the then Minister of Transport, Barbara Castle, to the effect that the section of the line between Bury and Rawtenstall had been reprieved.

However, whilst a reprieve had been granted for the line going up as far as Rawtenstall, this did not extend to Bacup. On Saturday, 3 December 1966, the 11.45 pm train from Rawtenstall - packed with enthusiasts and local people - was the last to run to Bacup.

There was a certain sting in the tail though as far as the 'reprieve' of the Bury-Rawtenstall section was concerned with BR now timetabling the stretch of line to operate with much reduced frequency. Having thought it had won the battle outright, the Summerseat-based action group now found itself engaged in protesting against the cuts in numbers of trains left operating. Campaigners could only think the new truncated timetable was BR's way of taking backhanded revenge on local communities on the Bury-Rawtenstall line for having fought to retain their service.

In such circumstances, action group members decided to act more directly to demonstrate the strength of their renewed dissatisfaction. Plans were hatched in the latter months of 1966 to mount a major protest event at the start of the new year. On a cold Saturday in January 1967, a well-organised group of around 150 protesters turned up at Summerseat station for a public show of dissent.

The *Burnley Evening Star* chronicled happenings on the day by way of step-by-step build-up:

1.55 pm - Villagers, police and a BBC film team crowd the platform...demonstrators carry posters coloured shocking pink: '*Barbara Castle must go*' and '*Stop the train drain*'...

2.16 pm - The Rawtenstall-Bury train is now due. A woman walks on to the line…Two transport policewomen walk towards her…A man on the line is told by police: 'You are being reported for the offence of trespassing on the railway.'

2.25 pm - The train rolls into Summerseat to mixed cheers and jeers.

2.29 pm - It looks as if the train has cleared the demonstrators. But suddenly, at the last moment, the brakes go on as a man walks out from hiding to sit down on the rails a few feet from the train and forces a four minute halt to BR's new train schedule. The smell of success is in the air, as children sing: 'Where have all the trains gone?' [3]

Despite such newsworthy demonstrations, the future of the service continued in jeopardy. From March 1968 onwards, BR cost-saving exercises increasingly led to stations being unstaffed and vulnerable to vandalism. Further steps were taken a few months later towards line closure when BR began operating single-line operations on the route, with the disused second line being lifted for scrap.

Meanwhile, BR didn't lose sight of the tactical need to try and offset issues raised by Summerseat residents. At a public inquiry held on 29 October 1970, it was revealed that Bury Council was intent on spending £35,000 on road improvements, potentially enabling bus services to operate more effectively on the ground. The announcement was set to play a significant part by way of scotching Summerseat villagers' long-held argument that, without rail connection, the community would be exposed to social isolation.

'Ramsbottom station goes – and souvenir hunters move in.'
In spite of continuing protests, BR went on to propose the closure of the Bury to Rawtenstall line, the argument being put forward that the line was running at an annual loss of £95,000. This was clearly not accepted in Ramsbottom. For example, at a Ramsbottom District Council meeting, the proposal was disapproved with clerk Mr J. Alcock instructed to lodge a formal objection.[4]

However, with the die cast by the Government for the end of the Bury-Rawtenstall passenger service, the process of dismantling its infrastructure now went on apace. 1971 was to witness stations all along the track being demolished as a prelude to the closing of the line as a whole.

Once such a busy station, Ramsbottom had in its heyday a large staff, but ceased to be manned from 1968 onwards following the closure of the Accrington and Rawtenstall-Bacup lines. The closing-down of Ramsbottom station was announced and reported on in January 1971: 'The ticket office at Ramsbottom railway station is being taken down piece by piece this weekend. Within days it is likely there will be nothing left of the once busy station, opened in 1846.

'All that will stand on the platform is a temporary wooden shelter put up for passengers…The office is being taken down by hand because it is made of the best dressed stone…For many people, the station was not just a building…it was part of the character of the town.

'Already the souvenir hunters have been asking demolition workers for pieces of the station and signs so that it will not be forgotten altogether.

'The demolition has brought some surprises…Mr. Robert Willetts, a leading track man who has worked on the railways for 17 years found some tickets in the office dating as far back as 1888.

'Mr. Willetts, of Lime Grove, Ramsbottom, was helping to clear the office when he came across the tickets stuck behind a board. One dated April 1890 is a Lancashire and Yorkshire Railway ticket, third class from Bury to Ramsbottom. And the fare was fourpence.'[5]

Final reckoning for the Bury-Rawtenstall line

Summerseat, Stubbins, Ewood Bridge and Rawtenstall stations all suffered the same fate. Only Bury Bolton Street kept open. This was on account of the electric service which operated from Bury to Manchester. However, Bolton Street was by this point not a patch on its former self. The old ELR headquarter building had fallen into disuse and served as nothing more than a convenient storage facility for BR. The building which had been a style icon in its heyday was eventually deemed unsafe when, ultimately in 1974, the decision was taken to knock down the renowned one-time landmark.

A significant event, further marking the end of existing services, occurred at Ramsbottom with the ripping up of track to make the crossing a single line. Meanwhile, the demolition of stations acted as a telling precursor spelling the end for the Bury-Rawtenstall passenger line as a whole. In January 1972, its closure had been officially confirmed by the Minister of Transport. The announcement brought about further local derision, including recriminatory responses from Ramsbottom District Council:

'Chairman Councillor Albert Little told members during one meeting that "BR couldn't run the proverbial party in a brewery" while Councillor Herbert Mills made it clear in his view that "BR had set their stall out six years ago to run the service down". Councillor Little continued to challenge the quoted £95,000 per annum loss which BR said they were making on the line and rounded on BR for having refused to provide evidence for the figure when asked to do so'.

Criticism of the decision was not unanimous though. A defender of closure was Councillor David Johnson who stated that, from personal observation, the decision was justified given that "there were no more than four or five passengers on the train as a rule when it passed through Stubbins".[6]

By this point in proceedings, BR had given four months' notice of its intention to abandon the Bury-Rawtenstall line, announcing that the final trains would run on Saturday 3 June 1972. Having undoubtedly suffered declining numbers over the previous few years, it was ironic that the final train services on 3 June needed to be strengthened to a four-car unit to accommodate the hundreds of people who turned out to witness the parting of the last passenger train between Rawtenstall and Bury – the 9.05 pm.

There was added poignancy to the occasion with passenger facilities by this time having been reduced to a small wooden bus stop-style waiting shelter. For the travellers on this train, they were participating in a sad event marking the end of a 126-year long record of continuous passenger service. At the time, there seemed no reason to think there might ever arise opportunity to travel on the line again.

Meanwhile, freight trains continued to pass through Ramsbottom transporting coal to the depot at Rawtenstall. This service too was set to suffer closure in 1980 at a time of increasingly lower demand for coal, given that it was being replaced by gas and electricity as a source of fuel for both household and industrial purposes.

Formation of the East Lancashire Railway Preservation Society (ELRPS)

As successor to the original H&DRPS (Helmshore and District Railway Preservation Society) that had been formed in 1966, the ELRPS had kept plugging away from 1968 onwards, searching out possible ways of buying back the Stubbins/Accrington line off BR.

However, by Spring 1971, the Society finally had to accept that the goal of its home-grown project was unachievable. This realisation came after BR issued an ultimatum concerning the large sum of money (approaching £50,000 in total) they were requiring the Society to pay for the line together with the premises at Helmshore station. Richard Law, a Society member at the time, later recalled: 'the message BR sent out was "Buy it or move out!"

Over the next few months, a number of different alternative sites came under consideration. A way forward was recommended by Harry Brierley, a member of the Society, who spotted the potential of the Castlecroft goods warehouse at Bury Bolton Street station as a new base for the Society. Harry lived in Ramsbottom and travelled daily by train to Manchester, passing the Castlecroft site at the time it was being used by contractors building the Peel Way, part of the Bury bypass road system.

The yard surrounding the warehouse had been drastically reduced in size as a result of the road construction. However, the project was now complete with the site recently vacated by the contractors. There was still enough of the yard surviving though in which to put on events to attract public interest. The yard area was also well-sited in being adjacent to the Bury to Rawtenstall line. A further blessing came from gaining the support of Bury Council who let the ELRPS have the site on a peppercorn rent. In the aftermath of the closure of the Bury to Rawtenstall line in June 1972, the Society started to explore ways of taking over this line rather than the Stubbins to Accrington.

ELRPS vests its future in move to Castlecroft

The decision taken by the ELRPS to switch its base from Helmshore to Castlecroft amounted to a brave, adventurous step for the Society to have taken, not least in terms of also committing itself to re-opening the Bury-Rawtenstall line. As far as Ramsbottom was concerned, keeping to the positive side of things, the decision served to open up the outside possibility that events might yet happen to enable it to become a railway town once again.

Notes

1. *'The Reshaping of British Railways'*, pub. British Rail 1963, p.50
2. Michael Blakemore, *The Holcombe Brook Branch Line*, p.8
3. *Burnley Evening Star*, 16 January 1967
4. *Bury Times*, 23 June 1970
5. *Bury Times*, 9 January 1971
6. *Rossendale Free Press*, 5 February 1972

CHAPTER EIGHT -

'Heaven-sent opportunity': opening of the ELR heritage line in 1987

Salvaging the Bury-Rawtenstall Rail Track-Bed
Encouragingly in 1973 the ELRPS obtained from BR over a quarter of mile of track-bed alongside the Rawtenstall line. For the time being, the track had been laid and connected to the Museum yard, in the first instance offering longer footplate rides for steam rail enthusiasts.

At one point, the Society believed agreement had been reached in principle with local BR management to allow it to operate more broadly on the line. However, in August 1973, BR announced that its policy ruled out any preservation society being allowed to 'share' tracks, a reference to the continued use of the line to transport coal to the depot at Rawtenstall.

Ramsbottom Model Railway Club
With the demise of Ramsbottom station and train services no longer operating except for the freight train to Rawtenstall, it occurred to a small group of local rail enthusiasts who lived and/or worked within the town to follow through with an idea of their own to commemorate the life of Ramsbottom as a railway centre.

Thus the Ramsbottom Model Railway Club was founded in 1978. Its first meeting was held in the back room of Alan Garside's house in Rammy. 'The first chairman was Harry Dennis. Secretary was Norman Piper and Treasurer was Alan Garside.

'The first club house was based in the attic of the old Stubbins School located on Bolton Road North during 1978 but three months later the school was due to be demolished when Harry Dennis came across the present home at the Old Patmos Hall on Bury New Road. This building was the old Sunday School to the church of the same name that was located on the corner of Peel Brow and Bury New Road.

'The Club was able to purchase the building outright due to the members and friends all helping to purchase the building outright on the back of collecting waste paper and taking it down to the local paper mill which at that time paid people for waste paper.'[1]

The model railway itself was constructed to be a representation of Ramsbottom and its surrounding railway network as it would have looked in the 1950s. It was in 00 gauge and measured 33 feet by 15. Given that many of those involved were also members of Ramsbottom Cricket Club, it was decided that the cricket ground should be included.

By way of postscript, the Model Railway Club is still in business forty-five years later, as the author can confirm from having visited and talked with Alan Garside and John Walker. Present-day Chairman Alan Garside is always keen to welcome new members to meetings of the club, held on Thursday evenings at its long-established base on Bury New Road.

Hope grows for the return of 'reality rail'.
Meanwhile, although the memory of rail was being kept alive in different ways during the late 1970s, there had been few strong signs emerging up to this point of real-life 'reincarnation'. However, the closure of Bury's electric train service offered a glimmer of hope. The last such train had left Bury Bolton Street on 14 March 1980. The tracks were realigned over the weekend so that from Monday morning, trains from Manchester left the old route at Loco Junction, travelling a short way along the Bury Loop before curving sharply onto a new alignment leading to the island platform adjacent to the Bus Interchange.

The final 'godsend' though was delivered to the ELRPS in early December when it was announced that the coal goods train service to Rawtenstall would cease to operate. The closure had come about as the result of a general decline in the use of coal. Although, up to the 60s, coal had been the main fuel source for manufacturing businesses and also for heating domestic properties, gas usage had taken a strong hold through the 70s.

As Andrew Todd was later to recall: 'By the late 1970s, there were only one or two desultory diesels with a dozen trucks crawling up the line once or twice a week delivering coal to Rawtenstall. They only stopped at Ramsbottom whilst the signal boxes were unlocked by the crew so that the crossing gates could be opened and closed. An air of decrepitude and imminent mortality hung over the branch.'[2]

The final coal train to Rawtenstall ran on 5 December 1980, over eight years after passenger services had ended on the line, with No. *40098* given the honour of being the last locomotive to haul a freight train along the section of line through Heywood, Bury and Ramsbottom before terminating at Rawtenstall. Viewing the situation from a Society perspective though, it now had clear opportunity to step in to salvage the line for the purpose of operating its own passenger services.

The '*Rossendale Farewell Railtour*'

On Saturday 14 February 1981, the evocative sight of a passenger train had re-appeared on line, courtesy of a so-called '*Rossendale Farewell Railtour*' plying its way from Manchester Victoria to Rawtenstall. Using a six-coach DMU, the event had been organised by Rossendale-based rail enthusiast David Isherwood with a ticket price of £9.50. The train stopped off at Bury Bolton Street on the outward journey so that the 300 passengers could visit the Transport Museum.

Mindful of the importance of the Bolton Street site to any future Bury to Rawtenstall operation, the Society sought to gain assurances from local authorities that it was not about to be demolished. A meeting took place on 19 March 1981 involving representatives of the Society, BR and Greater Manchester, Lancashire, Bury and Rossendale Councils, at the end of which it was agreed that BR would protect the site and postpone lifting the track-line until at least August, allowing discussions to continue. There was no doubt that Council perceptions were beginning to change at this stage and that railway preservation was suddenly being seen as a potentially valuable tourist-trade amenity.

'The Phoenix' Rises: 1982 onwards

In an attempt to convince the local authorities that there was a demand for its proposed rail service, the Society successfully chartered a weekend event on the Bury to Rawtenstall line for the weekend of 27/28 March 1982. This special event coincided with the official closing of the original line ten years earlier. During these two days, an eight-car DMU ran three times from Bury Bolton Street to Rawtenstall.

The first departure took place at 10.30 am on the Saturday to the strains of *'See the Conquering Hero Come*s', the music that had welcomed the first ELR train to Bury in 1846. There were two coaches reserved for guests including councillors, council officers, BR officials and representatives of the North West Tourist Board.

The event had witnessed the appearance of ex-Manchester Ship Canal *0-6-0T 70*, officially named *'Phoenix'* for the purpose of the initiative. A total of 1,300 passengers travelled the route on the Saturday whilst more than 2,000 people were reported to have visited the museum.

Light at the End of the Tunnel?

A highly significant breakthrough though came on 9 November 1983 when the Greater Manchester Council, with Rossendale Council's approval, granted that the Bury to Rawtenstall line, offering positive prospects for Rammy, should be re-opened as a tourist amenity. The key enabling factor was the so-called *'Derelict Land Grant'* which presented Greater Manchester and Rossendale with the longer-term opportunity to recover from Central Government as much as £1.2 million out of their projected overall £1.7 million costs supporting the project.

The successful purchasing of the line came as a result of grant funding. In Spring 1984, the Department for the Environment directly awarded a Derelict Land Grant of £435,000 to Greater

Manchester Council and Rossendale Council to fund the purchase of the line from BR.

Thankfully, the two Councils consented to the purchase and then sanctioned a lease of the line for a period of 90 years to the East Lancashire Railway Trust – a body endowed with charitable status. The Board of nine members was to consist of three each from Greater Manchester, Rossendale Councils and the East Lancashire Railway Company. In relation to breaking news of the impending abolition of GMC, Keith Whitmore, chairing the GM Passenger Transport Authority at the time, later recalled how keen he was to move the heritage line project forward given that the GMC had so little time left in existence.

The ELR Trust was to administer the funds for the restoration and development of the railway, leasing the line and property from the local authorities which then leased on to the East Lancashire Light Railway Company. The ELLR Co was to be responsible for the day-to-day running of the railway and was the formal legal structure under which the Society worked. For its part, the ELRPS's members went on providing the volunteer labour force to cover the operation and maintenance of the railway plus a variety of other services such as publicity, catering and sales.

Meanwhile, the *Bury Transport Museum Journal* was boldly announcing that 'the Bury-Rawtenstall Line Re-opens Spring 1985'. This particular forecast was set to err rather on the optimistic side.[3]

Further issues to be resolved

In early 1986, complications arose with regard to a regulation called the *'Light Railway Order'*. This needed to be passed before the Society could be granted the right to operate services. However, the purchase of the railway from BR was not yet completed before news had broken that Greater Manchester Council was soon to be abolished. The GMC had to this point proved most supportive as to what ELRPS was seeking to achieve. Thankfully, most of GMC's functions devolved to the Metropolitan Borough of Bury Council which would in future also prove itself very much in tune with the Society's objectives.

Another *Derelict Land Grant* was awarded during the course of 1986 to Bury and Rossendale Councils, this time for £600,000. The money was provided to allow structures along the line to be restored to acceptable standards of working practice. Following years of neglect, the line was indeed in a run-down condition. For example, four bridges needed to be replaced between Ramsbottom and Rawtenstall whilst the stations themselves at those two important locations were virtually non-existent by now. The argument seemed irrefutable that the line had by this stage degenerated into 'derelict land'.

The Green Light Given

In Autumn 1986, all of the legal paperwork had been completed and 'Bury-Ramsbottom' was formally signed over from BR and the line then leased to East Lancashire Light Railway Co. Limited. After 18 years and countless setbacks, the ELRPS and its army of volunteers could justifiably feel confident that the company's core ambition had been achieved.

The green light had been given. It now meant that work could go forward by way of operating trains to Ramsbottom. Several logistical tasks needed to be undertaken in the meantime. For example, volunteers had their work cut out stabilising an area just to the south of Summerseat station which had a historical problem with landslips. It was not until Saturday 27 December 1986 that the *Sentinel* shunter, the works train venturing up the line as far as Summerseat, was able to undertake the remedial track-work necessary to enable driver training and familiarisation runs to take place.

Contractors had been hired to drain Square Reservoir viaduct just south of Ramsbottom, replacing it with a plain embankment. Meanwhile, the installation of the points and crossings forming the loops at Bury and Ramsbottom was taken on by the Society's volunteer force with a helping hand from a *Manpower Services Commission* team.

The ELR Locomotive and Carriage & Wagon Department had put in considerable work from 1985 onwards, in particular subjecting two of the Company's engines, ex-Central Electricity Gas Board (CEGB) '*No. 1*' and '*Bickershaw*' to the most rigorous examination and repair. The privately-owned *'Gothenburg'* received similar attention.

The Signalling Engineering Department, led by Peter Duncan, carried out installation of signalling at Bury and Ramsbottom. A lot of other work had to be undertaken to prepare Ramsbottom station for re-opening. Over fifteen years had elapsed since passenger services had been withdrawn from the Bury to Rawtenstall line back on 3 June 1972 and nearly seven since the last coal train had passed along the line on 5 December 1980.

Ramsbottom station, in order to render it fit for purpose at this stage, had had to have its long-neglected platform re-flagged, as well as being extended by a further two coach lengths to allow six coach trains to be accommodated. A run round loop was constructed alongside the platform. Meanwhile, level crossing and signal box provision could be deferred until the line was extended to Rawtenstall. A temporary portable building was put up, containing a waiting room, toilets and a small booking office. More permanent station facilities were set to follow, including a water tower.

Further delay encountered

Despite the tremendous amount of work and effort being put in, opening-date targets continued to be rather too optimistically projected. It was stated in the Society newsletter for November/December that the line would re-open on 6 June. However this target, like others before it, proved overly ambitious. Following a visit from Major Olver of the Railway Inspectorate in April, it had been recommended that the proposed opening date be put back to the end of July.

Re-opening of ELR line from Bury to Ramsbottom

The long anticipated 're-opening' eventually came about on the morning of Saturday 25 July. Preparations got underway at 10 a.m. when the two steam locomotives, *ELR 'No. 1'* and *'Gothenburg'*, double-headed a train consisting of six maroon *Mark One* coaches from Buckley Wells to Bury Bolton Street station. The driver of *ELR 'No.1'* was Phil Southern, whilst Ian Riley drove his own engine *'Gothenburg'*.

At Bury, 339 invited guests and dignitaries had been welcomed at the main entrance by Station Master Harry Hatcher before assembling on platform 3 and 4. Entertainment to mark the big day was provided by the *Irwell Forge Band*. At 10.20, the Mayor of Bury, Councillor Mrs Jacqui Adler, arrived to be welcomed by Trevor Jones, chairman of the EL Light Railway. Also present on the occasion was Mayor of Rossendale, Councillor Patrick Navin.

After the Mayor of Bury and Trevor Jones had addressed the assembled visitors, Councillor Adler signalled the train to run into platform 3. At 11 a.m., the Mayor gave the 'right away' with green flag and whistle from the vestibule-door window of the leading vehicle. To the strains of the band – and tumultuous cheering – the train embarked on its historic five-mile journey to Ramsbottom.

Arrival of the Train in Ramsbottom

The train arrived at Ramsbottom at 11.20 a.m., breaking through a celebratory banner strung across the platform. On alighting from their carriages, passengers were treated to further entertainment which was provided by the '*Clan Grant Pipe Band and Dancers*' hailing from Grantown-on-Spey situated about twenty miles south of Inverness in Scotland. There was a clear connection involved in inviting these performers from Speyside, given that it was the one-time stamping-ground of Ramsbottom's illustrious Grant family, who had lived there before migrating south to East Lancashire and becoming such prominent figures in Ramsbottom.

The Bury-Ramsbottom link on the day was conveyed at platform level by the coming together of respective Station Masters, Ramsbottom's Dave Greenwood and Bury's own legendary ELR stalwart, Harry Hatcher.

Two vintage open-top cars took leading guests up Bridge Street to a Chamber of Trade welcoming ceremony at the Old Market Place where the *Ramsbottom Steam Jazz Band* struck up a welcoming musical rendition. Dignitaries were then escorted back to the railway station to board the return train to Bury, setting off at 12.10. Lunch was provided at the *Castle Leisure Centre*.

The day was blessed with good weather throughout. A number of celebratory events had been put on in Ramsbottom such as a balloon race at midday. Also, there were charity displays and stalls in the market square and station car park. A fun fair was held in Nuttall Park and various activities took place at Holcombe Hill with the Peel Monument open for visitors during the day.

Further passenger trains left Bury at 1.30 pm, 3.00 pm, 4.30 pm and 6 pm. Whilst the first three were reserved for VIPs, later ones were available for members of the public with tickets purchased in advance at a price of £5.

In the evening, a free celebratory service was organised for the benefit of volunteers and members of the ELRPS, departing from Bury at 8.00 pm. More than 250 people made this trip to Ramsbottom. On the way back, the train stopped at Summerseat for travellers to enjoy an evening buffet at the *Waterside Inn*, provided by Society President Les Ratcliffe.

On the next day, although the weather was not so good, demand for train seats on the schedule was so great that an extra service was put on. The *Bury Times* quoted Trevor Jones, Chairman of the ELR, commenting on the success of the weekend as a whole: 'All the way along, we knew people appreciated the chance to have a service of this kind and wanted it. That has certainly been proved to be the case. It was just fantastic.'[4]

Influence of Trevor Jones

Born in 1945 into a railway family, Trevor's grandfather had been a signalman at Townsend Fold whilst his father had worked at Bacup Junction Box, later moving to Ramsbottom and then to Smithy Bridge near Rochdale.

As to what it meant to him personally, after having long ago become chairman of the railway company charged with the task of restoring the line, Trevor recalled: 'Twenty years ago we had 40 members and 80 feet of track…We've come a long way since then and we are going further with the new line and new stations. It brought home to me a bit back on a certain trip to London when

I stood on Euston station and saw our train to Ramsbottom up on the board with all the main line services.

With obvious sense of pride, Trevor added: 'I felt it was showing to the world that we were doing our bit. It brought a lump to my throat I can tell you.'[5]

Reactions in Rammy to re-opening of rail line
Ramsbottom had suffered in recent years from the severe economic downturn following on from the decline of traditional industries such as cotton. During the 70s and 80s, the town, like many others in East Lancashire, had begun to take on a run-down appearance, characterised by disused mills and boarded-up shops. Unquestionably, there was a sense of optimism in very many quarters with regard to the positive effect the restored railway service might have on the town and its surrounding area.

For example, Mrs Barbara Palmer, President of the *Ramsbottom Chamber of Trade*, remarked: 'It is very much an experimental year as far as the railway and Ramsbottom goes but this seems an easy and ideal way to promote the area. A boom in tourism centred on the town may seem a novel idea but it is not impossible…'

A *Bury Times* report continued: 'Her comments came at a packed special meeting to discuss the effect on the town. As well, suggestions for the provision of car parks and Sunday trading were discussed and the *Ramsbottom Heritage Society* put forward an idea for a tourist information centre.

'Mr Bert Bullough, a planning department official at Bury Council welcomed the suggestions and said that Ramsbottom is a key location in the railway development and should be promoted to its full potential. "Not only do we want to attract tourists but also walkers and ramblers. We are in the early stages of a very exciting tourism strategy for the whole borough and much of this is centred on the railway".

'However, Ramsbottom Labour councillor Brian Rigby advised caution over the development of Ramsbottom as a tourist centre: "There is a lot of scope for tourism in the area and I welcome the money it will generate and possible new employment. But we have to be careful not to overdevelop and destroy the town's olde-world charm. Do we want a Blackpool or do we want Ramsbottom?" [6]

Similarly, two contrasting sides to the argument were demonstrated at meetings of the *Ramsbottom Heritage Society* during the course of 1987. At a RHS meeting held in mid-May, the visiting speaker Barry Worthington, author of '*The Coming of Steam*', summarised his message to the town in the following way – 'For the future, it is obvious that the coming of the railway must affect our town. It is up to us all, and in particular the traders, to take advantage of this heaven-sent opportunity.' [7]

A more sanguine message however was delivered at the next RHS meeting on 8 July 1987. The speaker that evening, Chris Johnson, owner of the town's *Village Restaurant*, 'and an entrepreneur of some standing' said 'he noted the concern of many people that the town might be turned into a touristic nightmare of cafes, take-aways, tacky souvenir shops with litter-ridden streets. Whilst we could not live in a vacuum, surely it is the existing charm of Rammy that people are already drawn to… Large concerns are interested in development, but this would not help our small old-style shops, and gradually the essence of Ramsbottom would fade away.' [8]

Meanwhile, following on from the re-opening of the line, the ELR was keen to move things forward. One initiative was '*Santa Specials*' – trains to run at Christmas aimed amongst other things at enticing shoppers to Ramsbottom. '*Santa Specials*' duly took place through December with a gift from Father Christmas for all children a main feature of the occasion. Over 8,000 passengers availed themselves of the seasonal experience.

By the end of the year, 35,000 people had travelled along the four-mile stretch between Bury and Ramsbottom. One interesting side-effect though had been the number of people from Ramsbottom who used the service to go shopping in Bury. This even caused the local bus operation, *GM Buses*, to reduce its fares between Ramsbottom and Bury from £1.50 to £1.10 in face of the new competition. During 1988, the number of passengers travelling on the railway was set to increase to 60,000.

Whatever the speculation at the time as to whether the return of the railway would come as a benefit to the town or not, findings were to prove fairly conclusive down the line. As Andrew Todd was later to recall: 'With hindsight from 1992 the 80s saw Ramsbottom's biggest change this century – evolution from a declining industrial town on the margin of Bury to a bijou weekend tourist attraction. In the late 70s, once the Saturday morning shopping had finished, there was near-desertion of the streets (apart from the evening pub-goers) until Monday morning. The town got its market back in 1984 – it struggled at first, and was on some wintry Saturdays down to five stalls. But once the railway reopened, it was secure…The reopening to steam heritage on 25 July probably led to as big a change to the town as the initial opening had in 1846.'[9]

Ramsbottom to Carlisle

The first railtour to operate off the ELR line had run on 19 September 1987 when *'The Rossendale Valley Ltd'* travelled from Ramsbottom to Carlisle. ELR *'No. 1'* hauled the nine-coach train from Ramsbottom to Bury, arriving at 8.40 am, before a BR locomotive took over for the next leg of the tour conveying 320 or so passengers onwards. Travelling in nine carriages, an estimated 70% of travellers hailed from Ramsbottom.

Significantly, the trip on the scenic Settle/Carlisle line marked the first occasion for 21 years that a steam-hauled passenger train had linked up with BR lines for such an event. The return trip, going via Preston, left Carlisle at 5.20 pm arriving back in Rammy four hours later to round off a historic day all-round.

'East Lancashire Executive'

A further highly innovative step was taken on 7 November 1987 with the *Southern Electric Group* organising a tour from London Euston, which was given the heading *'East Lancashire Executive'*. This was the first charter excursion train that had journeyed from the British Rail network onto the ELR line since re-opening to passengers in July.

Upon arrival at Bury Bolton Street, the BR *Class 47* gave way to ELR traction, with *D832* and *40145* operating either side of the ten-coach train, *D832* leading from Bury to Ramsbottom. Passengers were able to spend time looking around Ramsbottom before returning to Bury, with *40145* leading the return working. Beyond this point, the railtour made its way back down the Bury to Manchester line. The tour also took in a selection of other local lines en route before heading back to London Euston. It proved a successful venture all-round and one which demonstrated ELR's capacity to play host to incoming railtours whilst at the same time offering an interesting addition to the Company's schedule of events.

New station at Ramsbottom
In order to allow necessary work to be carried out along the line during January and February, standard rail service was cut back. The ELR recognised that with the next goal in mind to extend the line to Rawtenstall, the Company needed to carry out a major programme of improvements to facilities at Ramsbottom station.

Firstly, a new water tower was erected to assist in powering steam locomotives working on the railway. Capable of holding 2,500 gallons of water, the fabrication work was carried out by volunteers Ian Riley and Alan Schofield. The water tower was moved to Ramsbottom by train, with a crane brought in to lift the tower into position on the platform.

Building work on the new permanent station started in 1988 at a cost of £90,000. Local tradesman Fred Rothwell, living on Dundee Lane, eventually came to be assigned the job when the original builder went bankrupt after only completing the foundation. Employing a 14-strong workforce, the eldest of whom was father-in-law Harry Davenport in his 70s, Fred commented: 'This contract means a lot to us, especially as this is my home town.' [10]

Apart from the centre of Ramsbottom town now becoming accessible to tourists travelling by rail, it was also seen necessary to offer ways and means of promoting other nearby attractions. This led to the establishment of a connecting bus service. In 1988, Rossendale Transport Limited gained the *Greater Manchester PTE* contract to operate the *476 'Ramsbottom Rover'* service between Ramsbottom station and Helmshore Textile Museum/Clough Head Quarry, via Holcombe Village.

The re-opened railway station received official stamp of approval in a civic ceremony on 19 June 1989 conducted by 'His Worship the Mayor of Bury Metropolitan Borough, Councillor Alan Matthews'. The new station was designed by Bury Council architect, Steven Lever, in a style sympathetic to that of 'original ELR' engineer JS Perring back in the 1840s. It featured an entrance hall, shop, booking office and kitchen area, plus a waiting room together with toilet facilities. Subsequently, 'society officials were delighted to learn that Ramsbottom station had been *"Highly Commended"* by the judges in the *1989 Ian Allan Railway Heritage Award'*. [11]

Bearing in mind existing plans to extend the line to Rawtenstall, work started on making Ramsbottom suitable for its new role as a through station with provision for two platforms, full signalling, and a loop for trains to pass each other. Between 8 and 10 July, a road closure was put in place on Bridge Street to allow the rails over the level crossing to be replaced and the road re-surfaced to reinstate the level crossing for double-track operations. Ducting and signal cabling, instigated by Peter Duncan and installed beneath the crossing, was successfully completed in time for the road to be re-opened according to schedule. The second platform was built later in the year and the footbridge (which transferred from the Dinting Railway Centre in Glossop, following its closure) installed between Christmas and the New Year with the aid of a 50-ton steam crane to place it imposingly over the track.

Notes
1. *'About Us'* – Ramsbottom Model Railway Club Website 2022
2. Andrew Todd – Foreword to Vol 1 of *Ramsbottom Reminiscences* (1992) p.7
3. Winter/Spring 1984 edition of the Bury Transport Museum Journal p.5
4. *Bury Times*, 28 June 1987
5. *Lancashire Life*, September 1988
6. *Bury Times*, 1 May 1987
7. *RHS Minutes* of Meeting held on 14 May 1987
8. *RHS Minutes* of Meeting held on 8 July 1987

9. Andrew Todd – Foreword to Vol 1 of *Ramsbottom Reminiscences* (1992) pp. 6-7
10. *Bury Times*, 13 January 1989
11. Summer/Autumn 1990 *ELR News Magazine* p.6

ELR 'No. 1' crosses Brooksbottom Viaduct August 1987

ELR 'No. 1' emerges from Nuttall Tunnel - August 1987

Newly re-opened Signal Box

Peter Duncan and David Steele carrying out installation work at level crossing

Brian Almond Ramsbottom Station Master
1987 - 97

View of Ramsbottom station with 'Leander' arriving in May 2007

Tour of Britain cyclists pass over level crossing - September 2019

Thomas the Tank Engine at ELR August 2023

Grant Coat-of-Arms on wall of Nuttall Hall Road cottages

David and Margaret Wilson at Summerseat Station

Andrew Todd in Ramsbottom signal box

Passing over of the pouch - photo taken in 2008.

Ramsbottom Station today

The author standing alongside Scotsman at Ramsbottom Station in 2023

Richard Law on the occasion of the 30-year anniversary of the ELRs re-opening, held in 2017

Chandra Law, current Station Master of Ramsbottom station

'Flying Scotswomen' 2023 - Chandra Law, Linda Henderson, Steph Elwood, Charlotte Instance, Beth Furness and Lesley Hampson Forefront: Amy Harbour of the NRM.

The bell from the original Ramsbottom Station

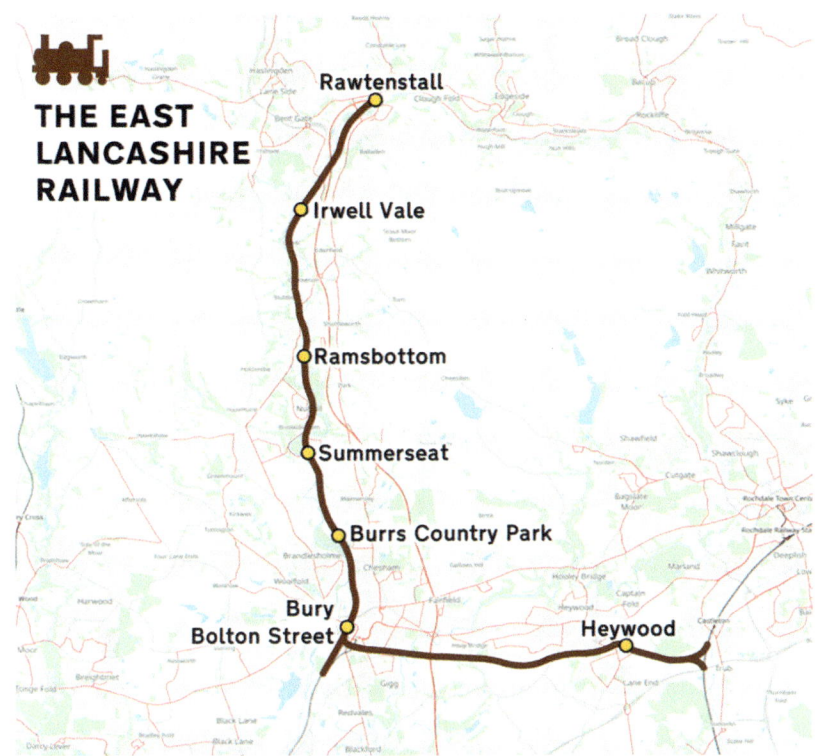

N.B. The initial connection in the ELR heritage line was created between Bury and Ramsbottom in 1987. The next link took place in 1991 with the line extending to Rawtenstall. In 2003, a subsequent link was established between Bury and Heywood. Although other stations had served as such on the original ELR route, the 'halt' at Burrs Country Park was newly created in 2016, honoured by the 'Flying Scotsman' opening operations there.

CHAPTER NINE –

Teddy Bear Picnics, *Thomas the Tank Engine* and *Santa Specials*

Delays in extending the ELR Ramsbottom-Rawtenstall line
In 1988, it had been brought to the public's notice that the Bury to Manchester electric railway line (described in the press as '*the end of the Leckies*') was to be replaced by a new Metrolink scheme.

Potentially, the new development was set to have an adverse effect in terms of isolating the ELR from the national rail network. This was because the platforms along the Metrolink route would need to be altered to accommodate the new light rail vehicles, making them unsuitable for the passage of standard railway rolling stock.

However, an alternative opportunity had appeared to open up to the ELR via potential use of a stretch of line between Heywood and Bury. Part of the former Rochdale-Bolton until it had closed to passenger services in October 1970, the line had been used by freight trains conveying coal to Rawtenstall until the end of 1980. A single line had remained in place in the meantime. Most of this appeared to be still in reasonably good condition.

Less positive news came in early February 1989 when it was announced that the planned extension of the passenger line from Ramsbottom to Rawtenstall, scheduled to take place during the August 1989 Bank Holiday weekend, had been postponed until at least Easter 1990. One reason for the delay was a series of modifications needing to be carried out to bring two other level crossings back into use – at Townsend Fold and Rawtenstall West. While this work was still underway, there also remained a number of other projects to be completed, such as the installation of replacement river bridges between Irwell Vale and Ewood Bridge, together with another on the approach to Rawtenstall.

Nuttall Park becomes natural home to the *'Teddy Bear's Picnic'* event

On a warm and sunny Bank Holiday on Monday 28 August 1989, the staging of a crowd-pleasing *'Teddy Bear's Picnic'* took place in Rammy's Nuttall Park. From this time onwards, it was set to become an annual event in the ELR calendar with a variety of family-friendly rides and attractions being put on. Added enticement was that all children accompanied by a teddy bear (and a fare-paying adult) travelled free of charge between Bury and Ramsbottom.

Upon arrival at Nuttall Park, 'children could enter their teddy bears for judging in one of four categories, namely – "*Best Teddy*", "*Trendiest Teddy*", "*Oldest Teddy*" and "*Most Unusual Teddy*". We expected a few hundred people but a few thousand arrived and travelled to the event on the railway'. [1]

Update on connecting with Rawtenstall

Despite disappointment felt from the postponement of the launch date of the passenger service to Rawtenstall, two working train services operated on Sunday 5 November 1989 by way of laying down a marker. The first service was hauled by former Burnley Gas Works *0-4-0ST 'No. 1'* in top-and-tail formation with *32 'Gothenburg'*, with a brake van and an LMS coach converted for engineers' use. The second train saw NWGB *'No. 1'* joined by ELR *8 'Sir Robert Peel'*, with two brake vans sandwiched between them, to allow as many ELR volunteers as possible to join the train through to the northern limit of the line. The priority going on into the 1990s though remained the re-establishment of the ELR extension line from Ramsbottom to Rawtenstall on a regular basis.

'Murder on the Ramsbottom Express'

In February 1990, 'tragedy' unfolded with a murder on the train from Bury to Ramsbottom. Fictionally-based on Agatha

Christie's 'Orient Express' tale, actors hired by the business company *Party Pieces* were dressed up for the occasion in 1920s fashions. A drama was staged with passengers having to work out 'whodunnit'. As quoted in an ELR magazine, it was 'one of the more unusual charters, requiring the provision of a body, a bottle of tomato ketchup and numerous pens and notepads.'[2]

Not long after, on 4 May, the ELR operated its first ever dining train: *'The Presidential Diner'*. The catering was organised by *Bury College Caterers* whose students and staff provided the food for the evening, with ELR volunteers serving wine and other drinks to diners.

Priced at £15.50 per person, inclusive of wine, the menu offered starters of pink grapefruit or prawns and salad. The main course was chicken breast stuffed with Parma ham and avocado with spring vegetables and new potatoes. For desserts, it was strawberry tartlet and cream, cheese and biscuits, and coffee to round off the repast.

The train made two return journeys between Bury and Ramsbottom as the 100 passengers made the most of the experience of dining on a steam train. The occasion was so successful that work began on the restoration of a Mar*k 1 SO* carriage for future events. The new facility would boast umber and cream livery, in a similar style to Pullman.

In June, the ELR launched its first midweek train service with a *'Schools Week'*, taking place 12/14 June. The three days were designed to give local children chance to enjoy a rail-ride experience and also visit nearby attractions. It was organised between the railway and local councils with input also from *Helmshore Textiles Museum* and *Rossendale Groundwork Trust*.

'Thomas – A Tank for All Seasons'

This talismanic event took root during the early 1990s, destined to become embedded in the ELR's calendar of events. At first, there had been mixed 'takes' at management level as to the wisdom of staging such an event. An article written by Malcolm Vickers posed the apparent dilemma:

'Previously held views on the ELR were that Thomas and everything associated with the Rev. W. Awdry's railway series was 'not for us' as an authentic preserved railway set in the late 50s/early 60s. It was against that background that the subject came to be raised again at the June council meeting in response to Brian Topping's repeated exhortations regarding the need for more events which would stimulate better attendance by the public'. [3]

Over the weekend of 22/23 September 1990, the ELR hosted its first *'Thomas the Tank Engine and Friends'* weekend. The former Meaford Power Station *0-6-OT ELR 'No. 1'* took the role of Thomas. In subsequent years, it was ex-Manchester Ship Canal *0-6-0 32 Gothenburg* that would be painted into Thomas' blue livery to play the part of the popular children's train-engine character.

Despite the Saturday proving a mixed day weather-wise, Malcolm Vickers reported 'it did not deter the visitors who came in their droves. By mid-afternoon, Bolton Street platforms 3 and 4 were packed with knowledgeable boys and girls, with mums and dads who had come to assess the quality and authenticity of the ELR Thomas the Tank offering.

'Not one, but many small souls castigated the *'Fat Controller'* for not wearing a yellow (instead of grey) waistcoat; we'll get it right next time! However, notwithstanding that small, but apparently important detail, everyone seemed to be entering into the spirit of the occasion, with the peddlers of Thomas tank engines, flags, whistles and other merchandise doing a roaring trade. At Ramsbottom, things were even busier.'

The inaugural *'Thomas Weekend'* proved a resounding success, with another 'first' for the ELR. All bar one of its operational steam locomotives had been in service, together with the running of three diesels. 'The station, operational and catering staff, loco crews and the public all reported that they had thoroughly enjoyed themselves. The booking office staff were also smiling with passenger numbers at 5,349, a record for a single weekend, proving that, indeed, Thomas is *"A Tank for All Seasons"*.

The 1991 follow-up proved equally successful overall even though 'controversy' arose regarding the casting of the *'Fat Controller'!* Although this year donning the correct yellow colour waistcoat, young *'Thomas'* enthusiasts now raised the different question: "Is he fat enough"?

'That's what all the youngsters visiting the event on Rammy platform were asking as the *'Fat Controller'* guided Thomas the Tank engine and his friends into the station.'⁴

It transpired that David Driver, playing the role on the day, had recently gone on a crash diet! Subjected to a weighing-scale assessment from Rammy Station Master Brian Almond, the inescapable conclusion was that he was now far too underweight to go on playing the part of *'Fat Controller'*.

Santa Specials

Back into the winter months of 1990, the ELR's successful *Santa Special* train set off from Bury with Brooksbottom Tunnel providing a particular source of excitement – hyped up in transit as the site of *Santa's Grotto*.

ELR Chairman Trevor Jones reported on the occasion: 'The *Specia*l pulled into Ramsbottom station packed to capacity with youngsters eager to meet Father Christmas. Each train pulls nine carriages, the normal number found on an intercity service. We must thank traders in Ramsbottom for doing a great job – it just shows what can be done for tourism in a short time.'⁵

More than anything, the event was about providing youngsters with a memorable experience. Certainly *'Poets' Platform'* illustrated this point with the publication of the following poem written by Paul Higson (age 11):

'The Santa Express'
The Santa Express on Christmas Eve
From Bury Station took its leave.
The children's faces, full of glee,
For Santa Claus they were about to see.
Steam appeared and the whistle blew.
Slowly but surely the train withdrew,
Under tunnels, steaming funnels
Wheels went round, engines pound.
As carriage by carriage passed Santa Claus,
Giving toys to girls and boys.

Waving happily he took his leave,
Saying, 'Go to bed early – it's Christmas Eve.'
The departure station is just round the bend,
Our fairy tale journey has come to an end
And, as the children went home to their beds
Memories of Santa Claus filled their heads. [6]

Opening of Ramsbottom to Rawtenstall line: 27 April 1991

The New Year into 1991 had heralded the start of two-train operations as the ELR geared up for re-opening through to Rawtenstall. The commissioning of the signalling, level crossing and extended run-round facilities at Ramsbottom towards the end of 1990 enabled trains to pass at the station for the first time. The running of two trains required ELR to fine-tune timetable details and also train staff to become used to operating trains on the new section of line. Although the restoration of the Ramsbottom to Rawtenstall stretch had not been without its problems and missed opening dates, the end target now lay within foreseeable reach.

After a set of familiarisation trips for training purposes, the long-awaited re-opening duly took place on Saturday 27 April 1991. The weather was fine and bright as the immaculately clean six-coach train, hauled by *0-6-0T 32 'Gothenburg'* and *0-6-0T ELR 'No. 1'* pulled into Platform 3 at Bury Bolton Street station, bursting through a celebratory banner set across the track. *32* was crewed by Terry Whitehouse and John Lewis, with Joe Strickleton and Malcolm Frost crewing *ELR 'No. 1'*.

As in 1987, the serving Mayor of Bury was called upon to wave off the first train. By a happy coincidence, it happened to be Councillor Monty Adler on duty on the day, husband of Councillor Jacqui Adler who had been Mayor of Bury when the official opening of the line to Ramsbottom had taken place four years earlier.

The train arrived at Ramsbottom where it was greeted by the *Haslingden and Helmshore Brass Band*. There was a scheduled 17-minute stop at the station, allowing time for various speeches and the topping-up of the two engines' water tanks. Meanwhile, the Mayor of Bury and his Rossendale counterpart, Councillor

Philip Dunne, unveiled a plaque at Ramsbottom station to commemorate the opening to Rawtenstall.

The plaque which can nowadays be viewed in Ramsbottom station waiting room reads as below:

TO COMMEMORATE THE RE-OPENING
OF THE
EAST LANCASHIRE RAILWAY
FROM
RAMSBOTTOM TO RAWTENSTALL
ON APRIL 27th 1991
MONTY ADLER   PHILIP DUNNE
MAYOR OF BURY   MAYOR OF ROSSENDALE

After departure from Ramsbottom, the train made its way to Rawtenstall, where another banner had been placed across the tracks to be broken through. The train was greeted tumultuously by hundreds of enthusiasts who had arrived to witness the event. Station master Dave Russell, having previously carried out the same role at Ramsbottom, was on hand to welcome the train and the dignitaries aboard. The *Water Brass Band* played the train into the station before vintage buses ferried guests to '*The Astoria*' for lunch.

Following the return of the celebratory re-opening train to Bury, an hourly service operated through the rest of the afternoon, with *32* and *ELR 'No. 1'* hauling the maroon six-coach train. Meanwhile, Derek Foster's BR *Standard 4 76079* and Ken Ryder's *7828 'Odney Manor'* took turns to be in charge of the second train, consisting of five carmine and cream *Mark One* coaches.

Pete Waterman and *Flying Scotsman*
Pete Waterman had enjoyed an active association with the ELR going back to 1988. TV personality and record producer, Pete had from early childhood been an ardent rail enthusiast. In more recent times, he had channelled his commercial gains into supporting local railway enterprises. In June 1988, his Class 25

diesel locomotive *25905* had made a notable contribution to the ELR's first *'Diesel Weekend'* held over 1/2 October 1988.

Since then, his collection of locomotives and rolling stock had grown considerably. During 1992, he bought two *Class 50* diesel locomotives off BR, the *50008 'Thunderer'* and *50015 'Valiant'*. Both were moved by rail to the Longsight Depot in Manchester, prior to transportation by road to Bury.

The two locomotives made their debut appearance, double-heading a Saturday afternoon service from Bury to Rawtenstall at the ELR's autumn diesel weekend taking place on 3/4 October. Both were to be looked after by the Manchester *Class 50* group. Also arriving at Bury in Autumn 1992 was a rake of six *Mark Two* carriages that were Pete Waterman purchases too.

In August, it was confirmed that the ELR would be one of only seven railways to host world-famous *LNER A3 Pacific locomotive 'Flying Scotsman'*, now part-owned by Pete Waterman. This was scheduled to take place throughout February 1993 with the train in steam each weekend, offering additional use on wine-and-dine services and footplate experiences.

Ramsbottom station wins another award

At a ceremony held on 8 January 1994, the ELR was again (after a similar success in 1987) presented with the prestigious *Association of Railway Preservation Society Award for 1993* in recognition of the railway's success in bringing together 18 locomotives at the summer Steam Festival event. Also that year, Ramsbottom Station Master Brian Almond, together with ELR Publicity Director, Graham Vevers and Steven Lever from Bury Council, had attended a ceremony at the Royal College of Arts in London to receive an *Ian Allan Heritage Award* in recognition of the transformation of Ramsbottom station.

Brian Almond's *A Day in the Life...*

By way of illustrating a Station Master's life, the following extracts are taken from a piece Brian Almond contributed to a copy of an ELR Magazine describing his day-to-day experience in the job:

'Oh no, more rain! I get up, shower, shave and take the twenty-minute walk through the wet fields to the station, arriving around seven o'clock. Having booked on, I start to get the scene set, bringing out the luggage and the trucks, fire buckets etc. – still getting wet (no canopy hint). Mind you, if the weather is still below freezing or it has been snowing, the platform, the crossing and the footbridge all have to be cleared, and I would light the brazier to unfreeze the water tower. This starts an eleven and a half to twelve hour day.

'Round about 7.30, a young lady from the market arrives with a cup of tea and a bacon sandwich. In winter, the first job afterwards is to set the fire in the Waiting Room, and then to start on the mopping and polishing.

'Around 8, the staff start to arrive, and we clear the tracks and platforms of any rubbish – still getting wet (no canopy hint, hint).

Between 9.30 and 9.40, signalmen begin to ring in from the three boxes at Rawtenstall West, Townsend Fold and Ramsbottom. I then ring Bury to confirm that we are manned.

'We have opened the station at around 9.30… I spend most of my time out on the platform, getting to meet the passengers and explaining about the railway and its surroundings. We seem to get a lot of people from abroad at Ramsbottom, mostly from the USA…

'I go through their jobs with staff. This involves sorting out who goes on which platform and who is to take the train staff to the box. With two trains arriving at the same time, we ideally need a minimum of two staff on each platform, safety being my main criterion at Ramsbottom. At this time, the platforms can get very busy bringing the elderly passengers and prams across the level crossing (so-called barrow crossing) rather than the footbridge.

'Once, the trains have departed, there's usually time for a brew and a laugh. Laughter is another criterion at Ramsbottom; we are a happy crew, as passengers will vouch for.

'If it's a fine day, I will have a look at the gardens. These areas are my pride and joy. You would be surprised at the number of customers who are interested in them and would like cuttings. I think bits of the garden must be sprouting all over England!

'When we get to teatime, one of the team nips out for chips (our staple diet) and somebody brews up again. As darkness falls, the electric lights and oil lamps on the station are all lit. Once the last train for Rawtenstall has left, we mop the toilets and generally tidy up. We do not usually have any passengers on the last train to Bury, but we leave room for them around the fire in the Waiting Room just in case.

'With the train ready for Bury and the staff on board, the final whistle ends another day in the life of a Station Master.'[7]

Postscript: Incidentally, the 'no canopy hint-hints' that Brian delivered in this account weren't destined to be acted upon during his time as Station Master, a canopy not being erected on platform until November 2006!

Rammy's *Peel Lions* on the right tracks
In May 1995, 'the first railway carriage in the country uniquely designed for disabled rail travellers had been launched on the ELR'. Up to this point, disabled people journeying on the Bury to Rawtenstall line had had to travel in the guard's van, separated from relatives and friends. From now on though, due to the active work put in by former ELR member Albert Potter together with gratefully-received financial support from *Peel Lions*, (the Ramsbottom-based charity organisation originally set up in 1974) were able to travel in a purpose-built facility.[8]

This new provision came with specially widened doors and electrically-operated ramps, a disabled toilet as well as a buffet and PA system. It had capacity to carry up to 18 wheelchairs with ten seats for other passengers, including helpers.

1996: '*150-year*' celebrations honour 1846 opening of ELR line.
Celebrating the opening of the original East Lancashire Railway line, which had taken place on 28 September 1846, a number of events were organised throughout August and September, with a VIP celebration taking place on 25 September 1996. The occasion started with speeches and presentations from officials on Platform 2 at Bury Bolton Street. ELRPS Chairman Harry Hatcher welcomed guests and then invited the Lord Lieutenant

of Greater Manchester, Colonel John Timmins, to unveil a plaque on the wall of the new café building on Platform 2.

At 13.15, the Mayor of Bury, Trevor Holt, on Platform 3, waved a green flag and blew a guard's whistle (loaned off Guard David Flood who, in accordance with the fashions of the 1840s, had acquired bushy sideburns and moustache for the occasion, together with Brian Almond sporting a top hat) to signal the 150th anniversary train's departure. Locomotives ex-L&Y *A class 0-6-0 1300* disguised as ELR *locomotive '150'* and Paddy Smith's *Black 5 No. 5407* double-headed the special train which had come from Buckley Wells.

The other main highlight on the day had been the formal handover at 12.45 of the National Railway Museum's Hughes-Fowler *'Crab' 2700*, the occasion being serenaded by the *Brass Band from Burnley Towneley High School*. The locomotive, which had spent a number of years assigned to Bury steam shed, had been placed on loan to the ELR. *2700* was handed over by the NRM's Head of Operations Ray Towell and a short ceremony took place on Platform 4 at Bury Bolton Street, with ELR Chairman Trevor Jones accepting the immaculate LMS lined-black liveried locomotive from the NRM.

The train departed at 1.30 pm and was paused on arrival at Ramsbottom so that travelling guests had chance both to visit the town and engage in conversation with a number of civic leaders and local business people. This was before moving on to Rawtenstall, where another plaque was unveiled, with ELRPS President Les Ratcliffe officiating. Guests partook of a special buffet lunch, served on board dining coaches that had been stabled in the bay platform at Rawtenstall earlier in the day.

Nuttall Tunnel and '*The Last Train*'

In September 1998, a Granada Television film crew descended on the ELR to film a science fiction drama, entitled '*The Last Train*', based around an end-of-world conflagration after a meteorite had struck the earth, with the only survivors being travellers happening to be passing through a railway tunnel at the time. 'As part of the filming, the northern end of Nuttall Tunnel was transformed with tonnes of rubbish and foliage to show a scene of devastation, leading to some local residents contacting the railway to report an incident of fly-tipping.' [9]

'Alex becomes youngest Station Master'
Sadly, Brian Almond felt a need to resign his post following a protracted period of ill-health. In the course of appointing a successor, the ELR had 'laid claim to having the youngest Station Master in railway preservation, following the appointment of 20-year-old Alex Walker to take charge of Ramsbottom station...Alex had been a volunteer on the railway for six years having started his ELR career helping out in the Bury Standard 4 Group shop at Bury Bolton Street. He had also trained to be a Guard at the age of 18, as well as being an established Booking Clerk...Meanwhile, Margaret Barber, who had been working to this point as Booking Office Manager at Ramsbottom, was promoted to Deputy Station Master.' [10]

Inauguration of *Railway at War Weekend* event
The 1999 May Bank Holiday weekend saw the ELR line transformed back in time to the 1940s with the holding of the first *'Railway at War Weekend'* event. Organised by Stations Administration Manager, Neil Parkington, the event succeeded brilliantly in staging a series of re-enactments and parades, as well as witnessing many attendees evoking the spirit of war-time by donning 1940s outfits and uniform.

The 1990s were certainly notable for the way in which Ramsbottom and the heritage line as a whole succeeded in meeting the challenge of 're-opening'. Many events starting out at this time, as well as becoming integral parts of the ELR's annual calendar into the future, most noticeably also affirmed Ramsbottom's resurrection as a railway town.

Notes
1. Winter/Spring 1990 *ELR News Magazine* p.7
2. Summer/Autumn 1990 *ELR News Magazine* p.6
3. Winter/Spring 1991 *ELR News Magazine* p. 26
4. *Rossendale Free Press*, 18 September 1991
5. *Bury Times*, 21 December 1991

6. Summer/Autumn *ELR News Magazine* 1990 p.22
7. Summer/Autumn *ELR News Magazine* 1995 pp.20-1
8. *Bury Times*, 5 May 1995
9. Andrew Coward, *The Revival of Railways in Bury and Rossendale – Back in Time: 1987-1999* – p. 198
10. As for Item above – p. 201

CHAPTER TEN -

Pride in maintaining Ramsbottom and Summerseat stations

The Wilsons and Summerseat
Much of the effort that had gone into the opening of the ELR heritage line in 1987 had understandably centred on putting trains back on track. Once operational, attention was given to appearance of station surrounds.

The *Winter/Spring 2000 ELR News Magazine*, a '*Stations Report*' – compiled by Andrew Coward – highlighted the work of an army of ELR volunteers intent on doing their utmost to improve the appearance of the grounds of various stations along the line. [1]

The transformation that for example Summerseat had undergone in recent years moved Margaret Wilson to write a poem in '*Poets Corner*' in tribute to the work her husband Dave had carried out there:

<u>Summerseat</u>
'Summerseat Station was a place not to see
All overgrown with brambles and so untidy
Of weeds there were plenty
But flowers were a rarity
Insects to bite and wasps to sting
But no pretty scene to make the heart sing
One man's quest to develop a garden
A mammoth task, Oh! Such a hard one

Every Sunday for four long years
He has dug and weeded and shed a few tears
He carried the stone piece by piece
To build the wall, to encase
Through rain, hail, snow and even the sun
He worked and worked, on and on
Determination and effort cannot be reckoned
But the garden so long, is it a record?
Now the garden is beautiful all through the year
And many a passenger gives him a cheer
As they trundled past in a comfortable carriage
Hauled by steam, diesel or DMU
Is one of them going to be you?
Come and see it, this station garden wonder
On the East Lancashire Railway
Where the engines thunder.' [2]

∞

The *'one man's quest'* described above had started for Dave Wilson after he and members of his family had ridden aboard *Flying Scotsman* in late June 1993. When on that occasion the train stopped at Summerseat, Dave, a keen gardener, had thought it a shame that the land surrounding the rail-track was so badly overgrown. After talking with Brian Almond, station master at Ramsbottom but who also had responsibility for the unmanned station at Summerseat, David had committed himself to seeking to 're-claim' the land.

'On the first Sunday during July', Dave was to recount in an article submitted later to the ELR Magazine, 'I met Roger Brierley, a member of the *Permanent Way* department, and one of the founders of the original garden at Summerseat, who received my explanation of what I thought needed doing with enthusiasm. Getting down to business, inspection revealed 'twelve-foot long tangled brambles, plantains, chickweed, rose bay willow herb, horse's tail and any number of grass varieties all trying, and in some places succeeding in strangling the life out of the more usual garden inhabitants.' [3]

At the end of his weekday work as an industrial chemist, and on Sunday mornings, Dave had subsequently made it his mission to tackle the invasive undergrowth and also reconstruct the station wall. The latter task had involved carting large piles of stone, stored in the goods shed at Brooksbottom viaduct, from a distance of some 300 sleepers down-line. He obviously did a good job on the area, the station gardens one year winning 2nd prize in the *'Bury in Bloom'* competition.

Meanwhile, Margaret, in her own right, had also carried out volunteer work in addition to her day job. Working as a Lecturer teaching Adult Basic Education at the Tyldesley section of Wigan College, she had enlisted with the ELR and served as Station Master at Bury Bolton Street (taking over from Harry Hatcher) for what would amount to a total of 17 years' period of service up until 2015.

History of Ramsbottom station masters since the re-opening of the heritage line in 1987

Brian Almond very much set the mould as far as dedicating himself to the welfare of Ramsbottom station was concerned. Not that it was ever plain-sailing. For example, Andrew Coward's *'Stations Report'* of 2000 also noted the threat posed to stations by acts of vandalism. It was reported how in recent times Brian had had to put in a lot of time 'checking which fencing panels had been damaged at the southern end of the station and with Stuart Walker carrying out regular repair work.'

Having started out in the job in 1987, Brian Almond's standing at Ramsbottom was already up there in local legend. Accolade had come his way in 1994 travelling down to the Royal College of Arts in London to receive an *Ian Allan Heritage Award* in recognition of the 'transformation of Ramsbottom station'.

Returning to *'Stations Report'*: 'It wasn't all bad news at this time at Rammy though, Andrew Coward noting that 'Chandra and Richard Law are now selling a range of 'Batik' gifts, as well as hot and cold drinks, and other items related to the themes of the railway'.[4]

Margaret Barber

In 2003, when the ELR line extended to Heywood, the *Rossendale Free Press* brought out an '8-page Souvenir Edition' to commemorate the event. It contained an article on the 'army of volunteers on track', making reference to the current Ramsbottom Station Master, Margaret Barber, as well as her husband Derek who carried out signalman duties.

'Married couple Margaret and Derek Barber share a passion of steam and railways with Station Master Margaret adding: "We have always been interested in the railway but when Derek retired from lorry-driving we had the time on our hands to volunteer, and we love it."

'I have been stationmaster for about two years now. I started working on the station, learning all the daily duties, then after five years became deputy stationmaster.

'It is a responsible job but I have a great staff…Margaret's team consists of station staff Bob McBeth, Barry Sale, Scott Cooper and Gill Johnson. Ron Hodkinson is the booking office supervisor and Chandra Law runs the station shop.'[5]

Chandra Law

For Chandra herself, these times marked the first chapter in a story that was eventually to see her following in the footsteps of Brian Almond and Margaret Barber to become Station Master at Ramsbottom in her own right. The circumstances behind this were somewhat unusual. In the case of most ELR volunteers, the decision to join up with the railway company usually stemmed back to some kind of strong local association in childhood.

However, in Chandra's case, her personal 'journey' to Ramsbottom railway station had taken a rather more complicated route, arising in essence from her husband-to-be Richard's work commitments abroad. Growing up as she did in Kuala Lumpur in Malaysia, Chandra confesses she hadn't had much cause to be interested in railways up to the point of 'happening to meet up with an Englishman who was involved in rail consultancy work out there.'

The 'Englishman' in question, Richard Law, had his roots in East Lancashire. Going back much earlier, Richard's family had moved to Helmshore when his father transferred from Darwen to become General Manager of the Rossendale Joint Transport Committee, which preceded the establishment of the Rossendale Borough Council in 1974.

Later, Richard worked for BR in a civil engineering post which, although based in Preston, involved his travelling around the country a lot, for example in London and Birmingham before moving north of the border to Scotland, putting in stints in Perth and Inverness in the mid-1970s. In the meantime though, he had kept his hand in working for the ELR as best he could, mostly at weekends, assisting in the restoration of old locomotives, coaches and track lay-out.

Then, during the course of the 1990s, Richard had taken on occasional consultancy work abroad, involving spells in Tbilisi in Georgia, plus going to the Far East to Bangkok, Hong Kong as well as Kuala Lumpur in Malaysia. Richard and Chandra had met there during 1997. On the completion of his contract, the two had settled in the UK. In Andrew Coward's *'News of 1998'*, it was recorded that 'volunteers on the railway celebrated the marriage of longstanding volunteer and ELR Operations Director, Richard Law, to his new wife Chandra.' [6]

While settling down to married life in East Lancashire, Chandra had carried out voluntary work for the ELR, involving a range of duties at Ramsbottom station, for example running the gift shop. Gradually though, she had become interested in the broader life of the station and in particular the managing of comings and goings of trains.

After Brian Almond had retired as station master in 1997, Chandra lent assistance to his various successors: Alex Walker, Margaret Barber, Stephen Lawton and Callum Stevens. Tackling training courses with the aim of becoming a station master, Chandra was destined to fulfil her ambition in the late 2010s.

1940s *'Wartime Weekend'* events - 2005 & 2008

2005 marked the 60th anniversary of both VE and VJ days. The occasion provided a bumper programme of commemorative events, probably the most notable being a Battle of Britain fly-past of vintage planes.

2008 was also a rather special year for three main reasons:

1. This year was the 40th Anniversary of the last steam train operated by British Railway.
2. It was the 10th year of the running of ELR's *Wartime Weekend*.
3. The year also coincided with the 40th Anniversary of the ELRPS.

There was no doubting the continued popularity of the annual occasion which succeeded in attracting thousands of visitors over the three days it ran, also including two evening dances. The ELR (with Neil Parkington continuing as chief co-ordinator) had become one of the leading national exponents of this type of event with visitors flocking here from all parts of the country. A large percentage were 're-enactors', entering into the wartime spirit by donning outfits from the 40s. For locals, it stood out as an out-of-the-ordinary experience walking along Bridge Street and beholding people dressed in uniform or wartime clothes from that period ('was that Winston Churchill I just saw?'), let alone rows of vintage vehicles on show.

The '*Rammy Rattler*'

Easter Saturday 7 April 2007 witnessed another unusual event when a specially chartered ELR train – the so-called '*Rammy Rattler*' – was commissioned by the football club *FC United of Manchester* to take 320 of its East Lancashire supporters' fan-base to travel to an away match against *Ramsbottom United*.

FC United of Manchester was a club that had been founded only two years earlier, in 2005, by a breakaway group of *Manchester United* fans who, despite the club's outstanding record of success over recent seasons, had become disillusioned at how they felt it had lost its local home-grown character along the way. Taken over by American businessman Malcolm Glazer, the new approach seemed just about making financial profit. This group of enthusiasts was seeking instead to create a club run on more local democratic lines, in a grass-roots style akin to how the original Newton Heath club had operated before changing identity to '*Manchester United*' back in 1902.

On 7 April, the '*Red Rebels*' boarded the train from Heywood onwards. Singing their hearts out during the match, the rail-travelling contingent of away supporters went home happy after their team had achieved the 2-1 victory that 'secured promotion to the Unibond Football League.' [7]

Despite Rams' Chairman Harry Williams being disappointed at the result, the blow was no doubt softened by a record gate of 1,653, swelling club coffers considerably.

An even bigger crowd, with away supporters again arriving courtesy of the *'Rammy Rattler'*, was to assemble for another special *Rammy United v FC United* fixture eight years later. 'This game, which took place on Saturday 4 April 2015, still stands as the record home attendance in Rammy United's history at 2,014...Winning 2-0 on the day, *FCUM* were destined to win the division that year, thereby gaining automatic promotion.' [8]

Irrespective of the distinctive circumstances of so-called 'Rammy Rattlers', spectators at *Ramsbottom United's* home games never fail to enjoy the sight of a train chugging its way along the stretch of track adjacent to the *Harry Williams Riverside Stadium*, tooting a horn or letting off a head of steam to lend added atmosphere to a match occasion.

The 20th Anniversary of the Re-opening of the Bury-Ramsbottom Line

A celebration lasting five days took place (25-29 July 2007) to mark 20 years since the re-opening of the Bury to Ramsbottom line. On Wednesday 25 July, a re-enactment train (11.05 departure), double-headed by *0-6-0ST's No. 70* (Manchester Ship Canal) and *No. 140* (National Coal Board) conveyed invited guests travelling in six carriages from Bolton Bury Street to Ramsbottom. A reception was held at Ramsbottom station with music played by the *Westwood Over-55s Brass Band*. A plaque was unveiled to mark the occasion before the train returned to Bury, followed by an event taking place in the *Elizabethan Suite* at Bury Town Hall.

During the rest of the day, and throughout Thursday 26 and Friday 27, in accordance with the 1987 timetable, the railway continued to operate a shuttle passenger service between Heywood and Bury. It was hauled by guest loco *3440 'City of Truro'* and from Bury to Ramsbottom using the two *0-6-0ST* tank locomotives and coaching stock. From Ramsbottom to Rawtenstall, a DMU service was in operation.

In the course of the five-day celebration, particular honour was bestowed on Trevor Jones who had died in November 2006. In his longstanding role as ELLR Co. Chairman, up to the time Peter Duncan took over responsibility in 2000, Trevor had undoubtedly been the driving-force behind the opening of the ELR heritage line between Bury and Ramsbottom in 1987, followed by extension of the route to Rawtenstall in 1991. The last official duty Trevor had performed was to meet a Chinese delegation at Ramsbottom station in May 2006. In honour of Trevor Jones' record of service over the years, a special ceremony was conducted during this week leading to an engine being named after him: *'East Lancashire Railway – Trevor Jones'*.

On Saturday 28 and Sunday 29 July, Ramsbottom station played host to a miniature railway for children's rides with other attractions on offer to visitors, including *Disco Dancing Demonstration, Funfair and Morris Dancing*. At Bury station, visitors had the chance to have a *'Standard Gauge Locomotive Driving Experience'* as well as there being Bury Transport Museum vehicles on display and a *'Thomas Event'* demonstration.

The 20th Anniversary celebrations were rounded off later in the year with an ELR Dance taking place on 17 November in the *Elizabethan Suite* at Bury Town Hall with music for *'Listening and Dancing'* provided by the Tommy Lowe Big Band and vocalist Don Graham.

30th Anniversary Event of 2017

On Tuesday 25 July, Ian Riley drove locomotive *'Gothenburg'* along the same stretch of track from Bury to Ramsbottom that he had famously driven the train along, 30 years earlier to the day, in the course of the historic re-opening of the line in 1987.

Sir William McAlpine (one-time owner of *'Flying Scotsman'* and currently chairman of the *Railway Heritage Trust*) unveiled a plaque on Ramsbottom station recording this 30th anniversary which, as David Layland said during the course of a commemorative speech, 'meant so much to all the rail pioneers who had taken the ELR on the journey to where it is today.'

A reception for the pioneers and invited guests was held at Bury Transport Museum. David Wright, Chairman of the ELRPS, greeting those present, took natural pride in recounting the many successes of the heritage railway company over the years.

Cycling Action Comes to Rammy
The Tour of Britain cycling event had first come to Ramsbottom in 2004. The next time occurred on 14 September 2019 when cyclists competing in the event that year pedalled hard over Bridge Street's level crossing with *Standard 4 locomotive 80080* standing by on track nearby to whistle encouragement to riders. Trains were re-timed on the day to ensure that the crossing would be clear when the cyclists raced through.

∞

However, inside the short space of the next few months, all such activities were fated to come to a sudden end as 'normal life' was reduced to a standstill with the onset of Covid lockdown measures in early 2020.

Notes
1. Winter/Spring 2000 *ELR News Magazine*, pp. 12-14
2. As for Item above, p. 38
3. Summer/Autumn 1998 *ELR News Magazine*, pp. 41-5
4. As for Item 1 above, p. 13
5. *Rossendale Free Press*, ELR Souvenir, 5 September 2003, p. 4
6. Andrew Coward, *Back In Time: 1987-1999*, p. 196
7. *Bury Times*, 12 April 2007
8. Nigel Jepson, *Come On You Rams*, 2020, pub. YouCaxton p. 127

CHAPTER ELEVEN –

Covid – during and after

Immediate effects of Covid pandemic
In the face of the outbreak of Covid-19, the ELR, including Rammy and its railway station, found itself put out of action by lockdown in the same way as all other business interests were at the time.

During 2020, ELRPS's then acting Chairman Chris Moore addressed members: 'To say we are living in testing times would be an understatement.

'In March this year, the railway entered a period of lockdown. Currently, we have no indication when it will re-open. Events we were all looking forward to have been cancelled or postponed. Not only is this disappointing to those who had planned to visit us, it also has an incredibly significant impact on the finances of the operating company due to the loss of revenue and the need to refund advance sales.' [1]

In business terms, the ELR suffered like others did. Visiting numbers that had peaked at 198,258 in 2019 plummeted to 22,249 over 2020 while recovery had only picked back up in 2021 to 100,000 on the strength of the end months of that year.

As seemed inevitable, figures drawn up retrospectively showed that the company's commercial viability came under increasing threat to the extent that a profit of £96,516 in 2019 translated into a loss of £34,808 in 2020. [2]

Walks round Nuttall Park during Covid

Lockdown was highly dispiriting in many ways. There was a strong sense of isolation from being largely confined inside the four walls of the house. One of the few consolations came in the form of the granting of an hour-long walk around the neighbourhood. As well as being able to take some exercise and breathe in fresh air, it acted as a psychological tonic. It also somehow made you take in the scenery with a keener eye. It was from going on these walks that I began to take much closer interest in local history.

At the time, my hour's walk tended to follow a fixed route, setting out from home on Bury New Road and heading down Nuttall Hall Road towards Nuttall Park. This developed into a routine, taking in a circuit of the park before veering off towards town, past the closed railway station and then heading back home.

One familiar sight missing from the park throughout this block of time was that of trains running round its edges. In other ways, such as the playground being out of commission, the atmosphere felt distinctly eerie. The search for things still left to see made one somehow become more vigilant. A case in point was spotting the crest on the front of the terraced cottages standing on the left-hand side of the road just before you reach the park. I'd passed these cottages many times pre-Covid without noticing it.

Catching sight of the crest prompted me to research the matter when I got back home. I discovered that these particular dwellings had been converted from Nuttall Hall's stable quarters into present-day cottage-form in 1902 but that the original Grant coat of arms (consisting of the fires on beacon hills of Craig Elachie north of the Cairngorms, three crowns and the words 'Stand fast') had been retained as a form of legacy on the frontage. [3]

Despite the evidence of the crest, it was hard to imagine that the nearby car park I was wandering through was the one-time stately site of Nuttall Hall. After falling into disrepair, it had been demolished in 1952. Going back in time long after John Grant's tenure, the mansion house and surrounding property had in 1928 passed into the hands of local industrialist, Austin Townsend Porritt.

Philanthropic by nature, Porritt had dedicated the surrounding land in 1936 - the present day park I was walking in - for community use in the form of different kinds of recreational provision, including for example the present-day tennis-courts and bowling greens. Nowadays, apart from a very enlightening information board put up by the *Ramsbottom Heritage Society* and the monument commemorating Porritt's land donation, other visible evidence relating to the original Hall's past is much harder to pick out.

Whilst walking round the park during these same times, it was further intriguing to try and tease out other such 'vanished references'. For example, peering up the hill to my left, I tried to imagine what it must have been like to have caught sight of Grants Tower from down here in the valley, close to rail trackside.

Emerging from Nuttall Tunnel, passengers would have been able to make out Grants Tower to their right. The 50-feet high four-storey construction, built by the Grant Brothers in the 1820s in honour of their revered parents William and Grace, would have dominated the skyline above the ridge of land called Top o' th' Hoof.

However, Grants Tower too, like Nuttall Hall, has long since vanished. Suffering chronic neglect and buffeted by relentless exposure to the elements, this one-time seminal local landmark had finally collapsed in 1944. Straining one's eyes to the skyline in the present day, a telecommunications mast now commands the view instead.

Is there anything from the past, I ended up asking myself, that is still today standing four-square? Yes, there is... the undiminished sight of the Peel Monument, massively prominent on the horizon of Holcombe Moor to the other side of the valley, provides reassuring such evidence.

Obsessed by the notion of 'vanished references', I found the thoughts inside my head dwelling so much on the past, during Covid, that time seemed locked into reverse mode instead of moving forward.

'Good to be back'

Despite pandemic restrictions seeming to go on interminably, an end to the crisis eventually came. Businesses like ELR gradually started operating again. In his chairman's 2022 Report, David Wright commented that: '2021 was challenging for us all… gladly, in April and May, trains began running again…And it was good to be back.' Sounding a cautionary note though, he stated: 'But the pandemic has left a fundamental legacy. Many people from all walks of life have sat down and posed the question: what do I want to do with my life? Some have changed how and where they work. Some have changed what they want to achieve.'[4]

Undoubtedly, the pandemic had the effect of causing ELR personnel – whether paid staff or volunteers – to re-appraise their work-life balance in light of the experience of the previous year and more. The ELR experience was typical of what was happening across the country as a whole. Covid had had major impact on day-to-day patterns of existence during the many long months of hardship and enforced inactivity. When the dust finally settled, people's reactions varied. But for sure, things were never going to be the same across the board as pre-Covid.

As ELLRCo Chairman Mike Kelly put it: 'Nationally, Covid has massively impacted on people's way of life and has, possibly forever, changed the way we risk assess our future engagement reactions with other people. Heritage railways generally have experienced reduced numbers of volunteers, with some not returning, shielding or simply new volunteers turning out to help in the running of services and events with more and more paid staff being drafted in to fill in the gaps.'[5]

For some, it did indeed lead to a stepping back from pre-Covid levels of commitment or in some cases not resuming involvement at all. For others, the eventual ending of restrictions could not have come quickly enough, affording a massive sense of relief at being allowed to pick up again on what they had enjoyed so much doing prior to the enforced spell of loss of involvement.

'Returning volunteers': Margaret and Dave Wilson

Seeking to make contact with some of the returning volunteers to gauge their own reaction, I arranged a visit to Summerseat station one Sunday to catch up with the lives of Margaret and Dave Wilson. It seemed strange in one sense to think that their original association with the location went back 30 years to their ride on the *Flying Scotsman* in 1993

Both agreed it felt great to be back. Where they live is a 20-mile journey away. Travel restrictions had of course been in force during the pandemic. Apart from anything else, it had worried them how the grounds might have deteriorated during the intervening months. Luckily, nothing had suffered too badly. Watching as the two of them went about their work again on site in hi-vis orange jackets, Margaret and Dave appeared every inch 'back in the zone'. The garden and the whole station surrounds were a blaze of colour, so pleasing to the eye and testament to their dedication to the job in hand.

A while later, Margaret informs me that a train is about to arrive which turns out to be *80097* heading this way from Rawtenstall. Though no-one alights from the carriages, I cannot help but think that passengers, sitting at their window-seats, were no doubt impressed by what they saw of the station and its setting.

Continuing on to Summerseat
After *80097* has departed, I say farewell to the Wilsons and make my way down the platform to where the path leads on towards Summerseat itself. Along the way, I come across a notice-board containing two newspaper articles dating back to protests against the proposed closure of the Bury-Rawtenstall line. One bears the headline: 'Rail Unrest in Summerseat', reporting on events in 1967 when two protesters on line ended up being taken into police custody. The second press cutting – 'Last Train Given Send Off' – gave description of the final train journey on the last day of operation back in 1972.

The path I am venturing along now veers at an angle away from the rail-track, entering into the housing development that has subsequently come into being after 1972. The sight of the Brooksbottom Viaduct is still though as majestic as ever. Soon after, I reach the road bridge across the Irwell, staring down into the waters below. On the right side of the bridge there once stood, until relatively recently, the *Waterside Inn*, a 200-year-old pub and one-time venue of many ELR celebratory occasions. Alas no longer. Following a tumultuous storm on Boxing Day, 26 December 2015 when the waters had risen to devastatingly high levels, both *Waterside* and the bridge it stood upon had crumbled under the onslaught.

Resuming my walk, I notice, beyond the end of the newly resurrected bridge, the tall impressive edifice standing on the site of the original Brooksbottoms Mill, once owned by John Robinson Kay in the 19th century. In later times, Joshua Hoyle had taken over as factory-owner. In 1967, 400 people had been employed at the mill. When the '*Brox*', as it was known locally, finally closed in 1978, it had quickly fallen into a state of disrepair until being taken on by housing developers and converted into the up-market residential development known now as '*The Spinnings*', providing witness to Summerseat's transformation in more recent times from an industrial to a residential character.

Walk down to Ramsbottom
At the time when lockdown restrictions ended, as if suffering a kind of withdrawal symptom, I found it difficult breaking free of my familiar Nuttall Park walk. If not daily, I maintained the habit two or three times a week. It was a thrilling moment the first time I caught sight again of a train, back on track again, chugging its way round the edges of the park.

Today, there is a connected purpose to the walk I am undertaking. I've arranged to visit Rammy railway station, thankfully up and running again, to meet with Station Master Chandra Law.

Assuming everything is still working to plan, the train that I've seen in the park will have reached the station by the time I arrive and since have set off to Rawtenstall giving me a 'window' to talk with Chandra about her job.

Leaving Nuttall Park, I circumvent the *Fedex* site (originally the Grants' Square Works). Further along the way, I reach the aptly-named Railway Road, at the end of which stands Ramsbottom station.

Visiting Ramsbottom station

It is clear from the start how enthusiastic Chandra is about what she does. Wearing her Station Master's cap and uniform with natural pride, she busies herself around the place as if railway life had always been in the DNA. The memory almost slips from mind that the previous time we had met, Chandra owned to the fact that she hadn't had much interest in railways until meeting up with husband-to-be Richard in Kuala Lumpur in the 1990s.

I am interested now in finding out more about what had stoked her ambition to become a Station Master. I already know about her having served a series of informal apprenticeships under various post-holders from Brian Almond onwards. Retracing her account of the training process she had gone through, Chandra suddenly breaks into a peal of laughter. It had been nerve-wracking enough, she recounts, to be undergoing the final stage of examination without also having to contend with the presence of a film-crew from a certain TV 'railway channel' recording the whole experience for the benefit of viewers! Happily, she had done herself full justice on the day and emerged with flying colours.

In professional manner, she takes me through all the various aspects of the job description of an ELR stationmaster. Then, breaking off for a moment, she snatches a glance at her watch to alert me to the fact she will soon need to get ready for the arrival of the next train wending its way here from Bury. Wondering how I might occupy myself in the meantime, Chandra seems to read my mind and says: 'Did you know there is a very interesting information display in our waiting room, telling you a lot about the history of the station?'

'No, I didn't', I confess, but was very interested to take a look.

'Ramsbottom Railway Station – Past and Present'

Set up within the confines of the waiting room, the information boards covering its walls are entitled: 'Interpreting Ramsbottom Railway Station – Past and Present'. The display has been compiled by Andrew Todd. Various illustrations capture the eye, supplemented by absorbing text to scan through.

Later on in the day, after combing through RHS magazines, I came to learn more about the circumstances behind how this display came into being in the first place, as follows: 'It was a gift from Ramsbottom Heritage Society to the ELR and their Ramsbottom staff to say thank you for allowing us to sell seven editions of the "Ramsbottom War News" on the station and the trains throughout the period from 2010 to 2017. The RHS group who compiled the 'War News' – Brenda Richards, Anne Mortimer, Ingrid Gouldsborough, Ros Kendall and Brenda Newth – had felt it was a great all-round experience during those times getting involved in selling the paper, dressed up as mill workers or similar in the process and having sold well over 1,000 each year at £1 a copy'.[6]

Anyway back to the boards themselves! Apart from everything else of interest on display, what I find most captivating to read - even if having to admit it may be becoming something of a personal hobby-horse - is the account of what happened to the stonework of the original station when it was dismantled in 1972. Here, I pick up on the story of how at the time it had been bought off British Rail by John Lawrence, manager of Ramsbottom Paper Mill, who had in mind for the stonework to be put to use to create a new house for himself and his family on the present site of 42, Bury New Road... by coincidence where Anna and I have lived since 2000.

As well as this, 'it is fascinating to discover how Ramsbottom used to be the most important intermediate station in the Bury-Bacup-Accrington area, once so large and so busy with goods traffic and passenger trains that the gates were closed to the road up to 180 times a day, and very surprising to learn that the nearby sidings had a capacity of over six hundred wagons'.

With regard to Andrew Todd himself, he had been the founding Chairman of the Ramsbottom Heritage Society in 1987, in the same year that the heritage railway line had re-opened. Living the experience first-hand, he and his wife Irene had been honoured guests in one of the carriages travelling on the inaugural ELR journey from Bury to Ramsbottom.

It happens also to be the case that for a good number of years Andrew has served as an ELR volunteer signalman. In fact, he is putting in a stint of service in the Signal Box today and he's kindly agreed for me to visit him there.

Station Master's duties on the platform

Meanwhile, Chandra has returned to inform me that 'the next train is about to arrive'. Venturing back out into the light again, two different trains are approaching the station, coming in opposite directions. The first, arriving from Bury, grinds to a halt, apparently waiting for the one coming from Rawtenstall to pass it on the other line of the double-track. Whilst this scene unfolds, Chandra has positioned herself in prime position on the platform to oversee what is happening in either direction, up and down the line.

From the glint in her eye, zealous in carrying out her role, there is no doubt she's in absolute charge as events proceed. Whilst cheerfully welcoming passengers alighting from train on to platform, she then confidently oversees the boarding on to the trains of those embarking on onward journeys.

Like clockwork, the process unfolds in a matter of minutes before the two trains (one steam and the other diesel) are off in opposite directions. Now they are both safely departed, and Chandra has had a chance to get her breath back, I ask: 'Was that fairly typical in terms of usual comings and goings?'

'Yes, it's always busy here,' she responds. 'Ramsbottom does the most business of all stations on the line. It also has the most visitors just passing by and coming to take a look from more of a tourist perspective. Because the experience is so much in demand, that's why there's a £2 platform ticket charge making it the only station on the ELR where this applies '

Thinking back to the years when Chandra had served as a team-member herself under a series of different station-masters, I ask her about her own current team. She names them individually – 'Martin Arden, Stephen Doleman, Stephen Drysdale, Sean Dowse, Alek Zablinskyj and Daniel Bell' – before adding: 'My job is made a lot more straightforward because of what they do to make things operate smoothly.'

Chandra says she remains in working contact with Alex Walker (referred to previously as the youngest ever to be appointed a station master on heritage lines) who now holds the post of Assessor, working for the ELR, offering guidance to and monitoring Chandra in carrying out her role at Ramsbottom station.

Meanwhile Richard Law continues working for the ELR in the role of Operations Director. His significant contribution to the company was honoured at a special presentation evening held in Bury on 20 October 2021 when he was presented with a gold award for dedicated 51-year long service.

I gratefully thank Chandra for having spared me the time on a busy day's schedule. For me, it's all part of learning about how Ramsbottom station operates. I then move in the direction of the signal box with the aim of learning more about how the process is transacted of two trains passing through the station virtually simultaneously.

Exploring Ramsbottom Signal Box
The present-day signal box site stands very close to where there would once have been a road toll box. That's going back in time to when factory-owners Peel and Yates had built the bridge across the Irwell around 1800. The present signal box I'm now approaching, brick and timber-built, is the latest in a number of at least three to have occupied this site. The 1875 L&YR stone cabin for example had been replaced by the 1938/9 LMS construction that one-time signalman Fred Hanson recalled with mixed feelings. That particular box had closed in December 1980 when the coal train to and from Rawtenstall ceased operations.

The most obvious aspect of the present-day signal box attracting the attention of road- and rail users alike is the big hand-wheel governing level-crossing operations. Although a fairly common mechanism in past times, it is extremely unusual to see a rather rudimentary-looking procedure like this still in practice nowadays, particularly on an A-road.

Even if more spacious no doubt than Fred Hanson's description of the old L&YR pre-1939 box as 'poky, a queer little hole', my first impression today, after climbing up the few steps to reach inside, is of very confined conditions within, added to the fact that the limited space available is almost entirely taken up by mechanical levers of one sort or another.

After exchanging initial greetings, I ask Andrew about his day so far. He says everything's gone well since starting out on his shift at 9 o'clock. It occurs to me it's a task similar to that of a lighthouse keeper. Not quite so isolated but hardly a job suited to anyone averse to long spells of solitude, even though I become increasingly aware during the course of the visit how often he is in touch with other people via telephone.

Andrew explains the purposes of all the various levers – red for signals, black for points, blue for point locks and brown for the level crossing. He quickly alerts me to the fact that *'The Great Western 5643* is about to arrive from Bury. Meanwhile, the 14.10 diesel, coming in the opposite direction from Rawtenstall, is due in at 14.24.

Explaining he has calls to make with various parties up and down the line, to make sure things are going to schedule, I occupy my time trying to tease out the logistics of what is happening. The route which the *5643* has taken to arrive here from Bury has been along double-track. However, its onward journey from Rammy to Rawtenstall is on single-track. This explains why the diesel has had to come through the gates first, before resting on the Up platform, allowing *5643* then to move off in the safe knowledge that it will now have sole occupation of the single down line. Complex-sounding but important to get right…not least if, like Andrew, you've the job of pulling the right levers at the right time!

Further to this, the synchronisation of opening and closing of the level-crossing gates to road-users is most interesting to observe. Just as Victorian travellers reputedly were frazzled by the delays caused them, so it's still possible in more modern times. At this point, I find myself reminded of having recently seen the film *'A Monster Calls'* (2016), including a four-minute scene taken on location on Bridge Street, Ramsbottom. In it, the star of the movie, Sigourney Weaver, driving a Volvo estate car, is held up at the railway gates. While waiting for the train to pass, as it happened a BR DMU, an emotional scene suddenly erupts between the character played by Weaver and her grandson, sitting next to her, adding considerably to the tension they are already feeling on account of being late for an important visit being made to a local hospital.

Above all else, it is of overwhelming importance that the two trains on line should pass each other safely. Andrew later tells me how on 26 January 1921, seventeen people had fatally been killed in a head-on collision on the Cambrian Railway's line between Newtown and Abermule in Montgomeryshire. This tragedy had prompted new regulations to be introduced, aimed at preventing the possibility of such a collision ever taking place again on a single track used by trains travelling in opposite directions.

With heightened concentration, I look on as Andrew now ventures outside the box. This is by way of 'meeting' the diesel heading towards the station from Rawtenstall. Reaching the end of the single line track, the diesel reduces its speed to a virtual crawl, which allows someone in the engine-area manually to pass a pouch-like object (sometimes referred to as 'staff') over into Andrew's hands.

After the diesel had then passed on to the double-track of rail, with the train from Bury subsequently switching on to the single line, Andrew makes sure the same pouch is transferred on to a crew member - 'usually it is the fireman' - of that train for its onward journey on to the single-line stretch of track to Rawtenstall. By this means, possession of the 'pouch' confers sole authority to travel on this section of the route, hence guaranteeing safe passage. Kevin Atkins, a Rammy ex-signalman writing in 1996, had described how the process was likened by the loco men to the passing over of 'the keys to the kingdom'. [7]

I ask what is actually inside the 'pouch'. Nothing fancy, it contains a steel disc bearing the inscription 'Ramsbottom to Rawtenstall', pithy and to the point.

Complex as the whole level-crossing procedure itself appeared, it was impressive to see how smoothly matters are conducted. Everyone involved knew exactly what was expected of them, testifying to the effectiveness of training programmes.

If it were on the national network, everything of this sort would of course be conducted electronically. But what I've witnessed in operation today not only commemorates how things were traditionally done in the past but also serves to show how capably a heritage line like the ELR succeeds in terms of carrying out such practices in the present day at the foot of Bridge Street, Ramsbottom.

Notes
1. Spring/Summer *ELR Review* 2020 p.6
2. Winter/Spring *ELR Review* 2023 p. 10
3. *Nuttall Park and the Porritt Legacy to Ramsbottom*, 2008, pub. RHS, p.16
4. Winter *ELR Review* 2022 p.6
5. As for Item 4, p.81
6. Spring/Summer *RHS magazine* edition 2020 pp. 4/5
7. Kevin Atkins, *A Day in the life of a Signalman,* an article in Summer/Autumn *ELR News Magazine,* 1996, p. 46

Postscript

Tributes to Brian Almond

On Saturday 14 May 2022, a video was filmed on the platform of Rawtenstall station recording the celebration of the third birthday of a youngster by the name of Edward Almond. As a present, his parents Michael and Danielle had taken him on a steam train ride on the ELR. During the course of the video, Edward is seen blowing a whistle, raising a green flag and shouting 'right away'.

The video carried with it a highly significant and emotive backstory. Three-year-old Edward was carrying out the procedure in an identical manner to that which his great-grandfather Brian Almond would have done during the time that he had worked as an ELR station-master.

In an article that was to appear in the *Lancashire Evening Telegraph*, Edward's dad, Michael Almond, said 'it seems like railway and trains "are in his blood". Going back four generations in family history, Edward's great-grandpa Brian had served as Station Master at Ramsbottom station on the ELR between 1987 and 1997. He had died in September 2019.

To honour his grandfather's ELR involvement, Michael and other members of the Almond family had approached the company to put up a plaque on a bench at Ramsbottom Station to remember Brian by. The request was duly granted. Michael added: 'As a result, I often take Edward to see his great-grandpa's bench at Ramsbottom and of course to see the trains departing.'

The plaque on the bench reads:

In loving memory of
Brian Almond
1942-2019
Station Master at Ramsbottom Station
1987-1997

Recalling his own childhood memories, Michael said: 'Since a young age, my Grandpa would take me to the station to help out so I have a lot of fond memories myself going down to the station as a kid. He had so many stories to tell, from firing *Flying Scotsman* to driving trains, all of which Edward won't hear from him...so I make sure I tell Edward his stories.

'It's great that Edward loves trains and can visit his great grandpa's bench...I'm also very much aware how important it is to get younger people interested as they may one day become volunteers which is imperative to the running of the ELR for generations to come.'[1]

'Return to Normal'
With the resumption of the heritage train service post-Covid, ELR Vice President Keith Whitmore reported that from Summer 2022 onwards, it had been a *'return to normal'* with *'Thomas Trains* running again...Well attended Diesel, Steam and DMU galas have also been able to return and the icing on the cake must be the privilege to be able to not only run *Flying Scotsman* along the line, but for visitors to board the footplate'.[2]

In addition, the *Dining with Distinction* programme was very much back in full swing. With Rammy playing a central part as ever in company events, the ELR was awarded the 2022 *Tripadvisor 'Travellers Choice Award'* for its *Dining with Distinction* service.

'Steampunk' at Ramsbottom
'Steampunk' was a ground-breaking event that took place on Saturday 28 and Sunday 29 May 2022, specifically geared around Ramsbottom station and surrounding town. For many, the question arose: What is *Steampunk?* The answer: 'a genre of science fiction that has a historical setting and typically features steam-powered machinery rather than advanced technology. *Steampunk* is a design style inspired by Victorian-era industrialism. Science fiction author K.W. Jeter created the term 'steampunk' in May 1987 to describe a style of fantasy fiction that featured Victorian technology powered by steam.'[3]

In similar fashion to how people dress up to attend *40s Weekends* (changed in name in recent times from '*War Weekends*'), many visitors to *Steampunk* came attired in a seeming fusion of Victorian and Goth styles. In the event, May 2022 proved a great success and the intention is to roll the event out across the whole 12 miles of the ELR in future.

Challenges lying ahead

ELR was named as a finalist in the prestigious *'Large Event of the Year'* category of the *Lancashire Tourism Awards* for its annual *Santa Special* events. ELR Chairman Mike Kelly commented: 'Our *Santa Specials*, the largest such event put on in the country by a heritage line, saw 42,000 people of all ages attending. Our aim each year is to make the event bigger and better in terms of bringing the Christmas magic and experience to the railway.' [4]

Meanwhile, by way of connecting up past and present, Mike Kelly added: 'In July, the ELR will celebrate 36 years of continuous operation and I am sure the challenges back in 1987 were no less daunting, as each throws up a mixture of year-on-year challenges but some unique ones that push us to extremes sometimes.' [5]

City Valley Link

One major 'challenge' emerging in recent times has come in the form of the '*City Valley Link*' proposal, a business case put forward by Rossendale Council with support from Lancashire County Council, arguing the need for a comprehensive railway system to be implemented to 'once again connect Rossendale and Lancashire'. This proposal carries with it clear implications as to possible changes coming about which might radically alter both the ELR as a heritage line and also the character of Ramsbottom as a railway town.

The case is based on perceived benefits to the local area through seeking to convert the existing heritage line into a commuter service, aimed in essence at providing an end-to-end journey of 44 minutes from Rawtenstall to Manchester Victoria, two trains per hour at peak times and one per hour in the off-peak.

In cost terms, the total sum for modification of the line, as well as making station improvements, weighs in at £80m, with an estimated annual operating cost in the region of £3-5m.

Outlined in two phases, the first phase of the *CVL* would use the existing heritage line between Rawtenstall and Bury. Phase 2 would use that between Bury (Market Street) via Heywood and then on to Manchester Victoria.

ELR Response to *CVL* proposals

Judging from Vice-President Keith Whitmore's response, as stated in the Winter 2020 *ELR Review*, he was decidedly against the project: 'At times it seems as if we are being used as a political football to prove a point to the Department of Transport, a meaningless political point and at the same time we are forced to defend our very existence rather than working with the Council to make Rawtenstall a worthy tourist destination. How many more times do we have to make the case that without the ELR we would never have seen the regeneration of Ramsbottom from a village that was really suffering from empty shop units and dereliction to the thriving tourist town which it is today. We will, I am afraid, have to keep up the pressure to ensure that these mad-capped ideas which threaten our very existence remain a line on a map never to see the light of day.'

ELR Chairman Mike Kelly stated further: 'It is our considered view that a new commuter line cannot co-exist with the existing ELR heritage line that our volunteers have given so much time and effort to preserve over the last 35 years.'[6]

Local Rammy reaction to *CVL* proposals

It is interesting to gauge local opinion to these new proposals. Below is a sample of reaction appearing on 'Wha*t*'s *On In Ramsbottom*' social media:
- 'Excellent news. We need more flexible transport solutions for locals and not just a tourist railway.
- 'Why would you want to invest in another public rail line into Manchester when the money could be more wisely spent elsewhere to improve the existing transport/road network.'

Postscript

- 'The heritage trains are lovely but we have to improve access to public transport.'
- 'This is so stupid - the east lancs brings the community together with its various events like the ghost train and santa specials.'
- 'I'll believe it when work starts. Another fairy tale proposal.'
- 'Some things need to move on. A commuter train would be a huge benefit to people in Rossendale and Ramsbottom.'
- 'With the increased number of people working from home compared to 3 years ago, it just doesn't seem worthwhile. Of course there are people who live in Rossendale that do work in Manchester but I very much doubt there is enough demand to make a profit.'
- 'I'm afraid that this is likely to be the start of the end of the East Lancs steam railway.'
- 'I'm sure something will happen in the next 10-15 years, the economic case for light rail bringing prosperity is quite well founded. How it interacts with ELR is the tricky part. I'd love to be able to catch the Metrolink from Rammy or Stubbins and not to have to drive to Whitefield. But I reckon I'll be close to retirement when it happens!'

Obviously, there are two sides to the coin as to the best way forward from this stage onwards. In the final analysis, as with most other multi-million pound proposals, funding streams and availability of finance are likely to prove vital factors regarding whether and/or when such a scheme as the *CVL* might come about in reality.

Draft *Ramsbottom Town Centre Plan*

Meanwhile, in December 2021, Bury Council had put forward a *Town Centre Plan* which in draft form sets out a series of short- and longer-term proposals intended to reduce conflict between pedestrians and vehicles, improve linkages between attractions, address parking issues for visitors and help business growth. Also included among the proposals are 'active travel initiatives' further facilitating links between town centre and the railway station. Again, it is a case of watch this space!

Maintenance of *Flying Scotsman* at the ELR in latter months of 2022

Since the heritage line opened in 1987, *Flying Scotsman* has on very many occasions proved a star attraction to ELR visitors of all ages.

During the latter months of 2022, I happened to be fortunate enough to come unexpectedly across the *Scotsman* on two separate occasions. The first was on the Buckley Wells site in Bury. Having gone there on other business, I was unaware even that the locomotive was temporarily being housed there undergoing maintenance work in advance of celebrating its centenary year in 2023.

On the day, at the end of a meeting, Andy Hardman, 'Traction and Rolling Stock' Deputy Head, mentioned *Scotsman's* presence on site to me and asked if I'd like to go and take a look. No second invitation needed!

Conducted to the shed where the work was being carried out, it gave me splendid opportunity to catch close-up sight of *Scotsman*. The job Andy carries out has naturally led him to concentrate more on the technical side of the engine's history. It was fascinating to listen to his account of all the changes and engine repairs carried out over the years, and tellingly at what expense to various owners. Catching sight of the *Scotsman* rested up, during a spell of hibernation, it felt a bit like taking advantage of someone when they were having a nap. Even in repose though, the locomotive still looked magnificent.

My second encounter, within a short matter of days, was again to come about by chance. Happening to be walking down to Rammy on a Saturday lunchtime looking for a bite to eat at a café, it was whilst passing the level crossing that I noticed one or two people standing there looking down the line as if something was about to happen. As far as I could tell the buzz was that the *Scotsman* was on the point of arriving at the station. Sure enough, within the next minute or two, the unmistakable form of the powerful green engine could be seen approaching where we were standing and then heaving to a smoke-billowing halt there on the platform.

Not allowing the consideration of a £2 ticket cost to stand in the way, I was determined to be there to witness its presence first-hand and at the same time make sure of catching a photo to celebrate the occasion.

It emerged later that the *Scotsman's* outing on the day had been kept 'secret' and not announced publicly for the purpose of allowing ELR staff to test out engine performance in the absence of overmuch public attention.

'Flying Scotswomen!'

With all necessary preparations having been carried out during the 'close season', the ELR programme burst back into action with a visit by *Scotsman* lasting from 1-25 March 2023.

One of the undoubted highlights of these 25 days took place on 8 March, marking *International Women's Day*, when *Flying Scotsman* hauled three round trips on the ELR with an all-female crew and cast, making it another first in its proud 100-year history.

Representing Rammy on the day was Chandra Law, keen as ever to do her best by the town and the ELR. Meanwhile, the ground-breaking all-women crew on the 8th March comprised the company's Linda Henderson (driver conductor), Charlotte Instance (cleaner), Steph Elwood (fireman), Lesley Hampson (guard) along with Beth Furness from Network Rail who drove the *A3*.

Linda Henderson (daughter of Dave and Margaret Wilson) had been just 14 when first volunteering at the ELR back in 1993 after travelling aboard the *Scotsman* on ELR lines with her mum, dad and younger brother. In subsequent years, Linda 'has taken on many different roles at the railway including dispatcher, signal operations manager and in March 2017 had become its first-ever female main line locomotive driver.'[7]

A last connection between 'past and present'

Yet another happening of a fortuitous nature, in line with my chance sightings of *Scotsman*, was set to take place and make a similar evocative impression.

At a stage of the research process when it seemed unlikely I was going to come across anything new, I was having lunch at Park Farm Café in Ramsbottom when owner/manager Judith Hilton, aware I was writing this book, mentioned that she knew someone who happened to be in possession of the bell from the original station built in 1846.

This turned out to be Jill Clough, the daughter of John Lawrence - one-time manager of the local paper mill - who it may be recalled had bought the station's stonework off BR in 1972 in order to build 42 Bury New Road for himself and his family. Jill informed me during the course of a phone conversation that the bell was an 'inheritance' she had acquired via her father John after he had died.

Whilst we were talking, it occurred to me to offer to 're-house' the bell alongside the original station stonework here at 42 Bury New Road. However, sensing how many fond memories it carried for Jill in relation to her father, I didn't. In the end, I felt grateful enough for Jill's kind offer to send me a photo of it to go by. In a symbolic kind of way, the image of the bell seemed to provide a final poignant symbol by way of connecting up 'past and present' aspects of the story of Ramsbottom as a railway town.

Notes

1. *'Young Bacup trainspotter steals hearts of hundreds in adorable video'* – *Lancashire Evening Telegraph*, 20 May 2022
2. Winter 2022 *ELR Review* p.15
3. Summer 2022 *ELR Review* p.36
4. *Bury Times*, 1 December 2022
5. Winter/Spring 2023 *ELRPS Magazine* p.18
6. Winter 2022 *ELR Review* p. 17
7. Brian Sharpe with Robin Jones, *The Flying Scotswomen!* – an article in *Flying Scotsman – Centenary Special*, pub. Mortons Media Group Ltd., p.143

Sources

Surprising Lancashire (Chris Aspin) published by Helmshore Local History Society 1988

Lancashire 1750 to 1850: The First Industrial Society (Chris Aspin) published by Carnegie 1995

Railways in East Lancashire (Martin Bairstow) published by Martin Bairstow 1988

The East *Lancashire Railway (Martin Bairstow) published by Martin Bairstow 1993*

Ramsbottom Volumes 1 & 2 (Ken Beetson) 1978

The Holcombe Brook Branch (Michael Blakemore) 1975

Opening of the East Lancashire (Bradshaw's Railway Gazette) 1846

The Decline of British Railways in Bury and Rossendale (Andrew Coward) published by Andrew Coward 2013

The Revival of Railways in Bury and Rossendale: Back in Time: 1987-1999 (Andrew Coward) published by Andrew Coward 2016

History of the English Railway 1820-45 – Volume II (John Francis) published 1851

The Railway Comes to Bury – Communication Developments in South-East Lancashire (Harry Hanson) 1969 BA dissertation, University of Manchester

Harrison and Sale's Guide to the East Lancashire Railway -1849

A Personal History of the East Lancashire Railway Preservation Society up to 2010 (Harry Hatcher) Unpublished – copy received courtesy of Peter Duncan (ELR Light Railway Company Chairman 2000-2015)

The Reshaping of British Railways (HMSO) 1963

The Holcombe Brook Branch – No. 6 in 'Branchlines of the L&YR' series, published by the L&YR Society 1988

The Bacup Branch (Ramsbottom-Stubbins-Rawtenstall) – No. 3 in 'Branchlines of the L&YR' series, published by the L&YR Society 1985

The Story of the "Cheeryble" Grants (William Hume Elliot) published by Sherratt and Hughes, Manchester, 1906

Come On You Rams (Nigel Jepson) published by YouCaxton 2020

175 Not Out (Nigel Jepson) published by YouCaxton 2022

Ramsbottom's Revolutionary Doctor (Nigel Jepson) published by YouCaxton Biography 2021

Memories of Nuttall Village (K. McCarthy) published by K. McCarthy 1992

Steam Trains Today: Journeys Along Britain's Heritage Railways (Andrew Martin) published by Profile Books 2022

Nuttall – Ramsbottom's Lost Village (Ramsbottom Heritage Society) 2020

Nuttall Park and the Porritt Legacy to Ramsbottom (Ramsbottom Heritage Society) 2008

Ramsbottom Reminiscences (Ramsbottom Heritage Society – edited by Andrew Todd) 2022

Flying Scotsman – Centenary Special (Brian Sharpe with Robin Jones) published by Mortons Media Group Ltd 2023

A History of Edenfield & District (John Simpson) published by Edenfield Local History Society 2003

Zeppelins Over Lancashire (Peter JC Smith) published by Neil Richardson 1991

Around Ramsbottom (Andrew Todd and the RHS) published by Chalford 1995

Railways In and Around Bury (Jeffrey Wells) published by Challenger 1995

East Lancashire Lines: Bury to Heywood and Rawtenstall (J Wells & EF Bentley) published by Foxline 2000

ELR magazine articles – courtesy of ELRPS volunteer Kevin Rouse (working at the Emporium at Bury Bolton Street station).

Newspaper articles from a range of sources including: *Manchester Guardian, Bury Times, Ramsbottom Observer, Rossendale Free Press, Accrington Observer, Bacup Times, Blackburn Standard, Burnley Evening Star*

Various other magazines including: *Lancashire Life, Railway Times*

Turnpike Trust Statements and Accounts

Manchester, Bury and Rossendale Railway Company minutes

Ramsbottom Heritage Society magazine articles

Ramsbottom Heritage Society relevant minutes of meetings – courtesy of RHS Secretary John Leyland

Copies of '*Ramsbottom War News*' (Life in Ramsbottom during WW2) - courtesy of RHS

City Valley Rail proposal – '*A Better Connected Local Economy: The Case For the City Valley Rail Link*' – Autumn 2022

'*What's on in Ramsbottom*'

'*About Us*' – Ramsbottom Model Railway Club

Forthcoming Publication

Watch out for the following publication in 2024 from the pen of this author…

If you have enjoyed reading 'The *Railway Town of Ramsbottom*', make sure you look out for a forthcoming book written by the same author, Nigel Jepson, entitled '*The East Lancashire Railway*', which is due out in 2024.

This book tells the further intriguing story of the two 'lives' of the East Lancashire Railway: the first from 1846 to 1859 and the second from 1987 as a heritage line. While '*The Railway Town of Ramsbottom*' has largely concentrated on the fortunes of one particular town/station, 'The *East Lancashire Railway*' takes a broader sweep, both in terms of examining railway developments across East Lancashire as a whole whilst also placing local developments within the context of the national scene from the time of Stephenson's '*Rocket*' onwards.

'T*he East Lancashire Railway*' presents evocative first-hand accounts to demonstrate the powerful effect that railway development, from the early 19th century to the present day, has had in influencing and shaping the lives of people across the whole of East Lancashire.

∞

'*The East Lancashire Railway*' provides the latest in a series of books written by author Nigel Jepson, each aimed at highlighting distinctive features of the history of the local area:
- '*The Railway Town of Ramsbottom: Past and Present*' (2023)
- '*175 Not Out: The Story of Ramsbottom Cricket Club*' (2022)
- '*Ramsbottom's Revolutionary Doctor: The Life and Times of Peter Murray McDouall*' (2021)
- '*Come on You Rams: The Story of Ramsbottom United Football Club*' (2020)

∞

WITHINGTON HOSPITAL COMMUNITY
ARRIVE 13.20
16 AUGUST 2024
DOROTHY KIRBY
RADIOLOGY BOOKING
OFFICE